Cardiff Central

Ten writers return to the Welsh capital

First impression – 2003

ISBN 1 84323 280 4

This book is published with the support of the
Welsh Books Council.

*Printed in Wales at
Gomer Press, Llandysul, Ceredigion SA44 4QL*

CONTENTS

FOREWORD

Someone, sometime, will be able to point to a month, a day, an hour, and say, confidently: 'Yes, that's it. That's when Cardiff *really* became a capital city in the minds of her writers and artists.' Literature and politics may have a habit of diverging just at the points when you might expect them to merge seamlessly into movements and trends, but the time and place that will surely stand out as central to the transformation of the city's literary landscape will be Cardiff City Hall on Friday 19th September, 1997. In the early hours of the morning, it was announced that the Welsh electorate had voted for devolution by a margin of just 1%.

That was six years ago, and there has been a surge of creativity from Wales's writers since then. While Valleys writing has remained a vital strand of Welsh fiction in English, with Richard John Evans's *Entertainment* and Rachel Trezise's *In and Out of the Goldfish Bowl* giving voice to post-industrial disaffection, an urban wave has emerged from the Welsh capital in the shape of what Tony Bianchi has called the *noir* novels of John Williams, Sean Burke and Trezza Azzopardi. What readers and critics alike seem to be enjoying about this new urban writing from Wales is that it is fresh, vibrant and yet distinctly Welsh; it is also recognisable and appealing to a non-Welsh audience (hence the interest from London publishers in fiction currently coming out of Wales). While critics are more hesitant about locating any such distinctly Welsh urban aesthetic in poetry – Richard Poole, for example, recently wondered what 'Wales World Poetry' is, exactly – it is clear from the success of groundbreaking collections such as Grahame Davies's *Cadwyni Rhyddid* (The Chains of Freedom) that Welsh urban writing is not limited to fiction alone. When *Cadwyni Rhyddid* won the Arts Council of Wales Book of the Year Award in 2002, it was hailed as the work of a new phenomenon – 'y bardd dinesig': an urban poet who combines the radical political ideals of traditional *gwerin* (primarily rural) Welsh poetry with a contemporary urban and satirical perspective.

It is ten years since I lived in Cardiff, and in that time the architectural landscape, just like the political and literary territory, has changed beyond recognition. As the developers have converted old malthouses in the Bay into luxury apartments, Cardiff's administrative leaders have created a contemporary vocabulary for the city which seeks to project an image of a positive, aspirational civic identity. Cardiff's recent bid to become Europe's Cultural Capital for 2008 was typical in this respect: the city's PR gurus selected and put their own spin on the words of playwright Ed Thomas ('Show me somewhere good . . .') in order to flag up the city's creative as well as cultural potential.

Amidst this flurry of changes, it is easy to get caught up in a fashionable, plastic image of Cardiff, and to risk forgetting the colourful, gritty history and identity of the city, just as it is all too easy to forget that Cardiff has always thrown up writers in many different styles and genres, not just the *noir* writers of the new urban wave. While I was associate editor of *Planet* between 1998 and 2001, editor John Barnie commissioned a series of articles by Peter Finch about Cardiff, articles which documented the city on the cusp of major change (Finch has since explored the city further in his book *Real Cardiff*, published by Seren Books in 2002). I was fascinated by Finch's very personal yet sophisticated approach. Here is a writer who seeks to tell it as it is, who refuses to dress Cardiff up for the cultural tourists. His mapping of the city is rooted both geographically and in historical terms: nonetheless, it is no textbook guide, as Finch relies as much upon anecdote, snippets of remembered information and random associations as upon names and dates. I wondered what would emerge if I brought together a group of writers for whom Cardiff is similarly central – either as the place of their birth, or as the place where they have spent a seminal period of time working and writing – and asked them to reflect upon their Cardiff in a piece of autobiography.

In the ten pieces gathered together in this anthology, the reader will discover and re-discover a place called Cardiff. This Cardiff is a palimpsest of remembered and imagined Cardiffs, each layer contributing to a unique and profound map of the city, its deep history, what Kaite O'Reilly calls the very 'membrane' of the place itself. It is for this reason that I have avoided placing the pieces in chronological order, as the connections that emerge between them are far more complex than those suggested by a chronological trajectory. O'Reilly, for example, both remembers the haunted house she lived in during the '90s and imagines the city as it was during the middle of the nineteenth century, when her Irish forefathers escaped the potato famine and found themselves alighting at Cardiff Docks. John Williams, on the other hand, focuses on a relatively short period of his youth, but nevertheless offers an insight into the development of his creative fascination with Cardiff's Docks as a social and creative hinterland which would become the location to which he would repeatedly return in his fiction. Grahame Davies, by contrast, uses personal memoir as an opportunity to trace his development as a political poet writing out of Cardiff.

Several of the writers 'promenade' around the city: they are modern-day *flâneurs* for whom autobiography is a constant re-invention of the self at every step. Similarly, the reader flits in and out of places during different eras and epochs: with Gillian Clarke and Kaite O'Reilly we wander past the Hayes Island Cafe in the '50s and '90s respectively; with Leonora Brito and Peter Finch we cover great swathes of the city, from Butetown to Llanrumney; and with Dannie Abse and Stella Levey we experience the bombings of the Second World War. Like many of the other writers included in this book, Lloyd Robson tramps around his territory, surveying the child that he was and the man that he has become, the disjuncture between then and now, and the problems that the writer faces in trying to fuse the present and the past in order to write himself 'whole'.

Through it all, shimmering in the near distance, are the 'tea-coloured waters of Cardiff Bay' described by Gwyneth Lewis in her contribution to the book, a reminder that Wales is a small country bounded mainly by sea. Notions of Welshness are not quite as fixed and immutable as it might be politically expedient for us to imagine them now. The ebb and flow of the Bristol Channel as it laps at the ankles of Cardiff's inhabitants can be seen as a metaphor for the shifts in the city's identity over the past hundred years or so, and the swirling, inexorable force of the tides is as strong as the pull of the past on the present in the autobiographies collected in *Cardiff Central*.

I began the process of commissioning this anthology while I was working as an editor for Gomer Press, and I am grateful to

Mairwen Prys Jones, Gomer's editorial director, for giving me the opportunity to complete the project on a freelance basis. I would also like to thank Ceri Wyn Jones, English-language editor at Gomer, for his support and assistance, and the Arts Council of Wales for the generous grant which enabled us to commission new work from some of Wales's foremost writers. Thanks must also go to John Barnie for suggesting the title of the book, and to Dannie Abse, from whom I borrowed the suggestive, elegiac resonances of the subtitle. Finally, I would like to thank the writers themselves for turning to the commission with such enthusiasm and thoughtful engagement. This is their book: this is their Cardiff.

Francesca Rhydderch
November 2003

NOTES ON THE AUTHORS

Dannie Abse's first collection of poetry was published in 1948 while he was still a medical student. Subsequent collections include *Selected Poems* (1970), which won a Welsh Arts Council Literature Award; *White Coat, Purple Coat: Collected Poems 1948–1988* (1989); and, most recently, *New and Collected Poems* (2003). He has also published plays and non-fiction, and has edited several poetry anthologies. *Goodbye, Twentieth Century* (2001) updates his first volume of autobiography, *A Poet in the Family* (1974). His novels include *Ash on a Young Man's Sleeve* (1954) and *The Strange Case of Dr Simmonds & Dr Glas*, which was longlisted for the Booker Prize in 2002. He is a fellow of the Royal Society of Literature and of the Welsh Academy.

Leonora Brito was born in Cardiff and grew up there. Her stories have been included in anthologies published by Penguin, Sheba and Parthian. Her collection of short stories, *Dat's Love,* was published by Seren in 1995.

Poet, writer, translator and playwright **Gillian Clarke** is President of Tŷ Newydd Writers' centre in Gwynedd, which she co-founded in 1990. A former editor of *The Anglo-Welsh Review,* her numerous poetry collections include *The Sundial* (1978), *The King of Britain's Daughter* (1993), *Five Fields* (1998) and *The Animal Wall and other poems* (for children) (1999). She is an Honorary Fellow of the University of Wales. Her next collection, *Making the Beds for the Dead*, is due from Carcanet in April 2004.

Grahame Davies's second volume of poetry, *Cadwyni Rhyddid*, won the Arts Council of Wales Book of the Year Award in 2002. In 1997, his first volume of poetry, *Adennill Tir*, won the Harri Webb Memorial Prize. Other publications include a literary anthology, *The Chosen People: Wales and the Jews* (2002), and *Ffiniau/ Borders,* a bilingual volume of poetry produced in collaboration with fellow poet Elin ap Hywel (2002).

Poet **Peter Finch** ran the Arts Council of Wales's specialist Oriel Bookshop in Cardiff between 1975 and 1998, and is now Chief Executive of Academi, the Welsh National Literature Promotion Agency and Society for Writers. His most recent collection of poetry is *Food* (2001). *Real Cardiff*, an alternative guidebook, history and literary ramble, was published in 2002. He is currently editing an anthology of post-1980 fiction and poetry, *The Big Book of Cardiff*, for Seren, and working on a book about the greater city, *Real Cardiff Two*.

Stella Schiller Levey was recently awarded a first-class honours degree in English Studies at the University of Glamorgan.

Bilingual poet **Gwyneth Lewis** was awarded a grant by the National Endowment for Science, Technology and the Arts (NESTA) in 2001 to sail to ports that are linked historically with Cardiff. Her first poetry collection in English, *Parables and Faxes* (1995), was shortlisted for the Forward Prize (Best First Collection). *Zero Gravity* (1998) was shortlisted for the Forward Poetry Prize (Best Collection), and *Y Llofrudd Iaith* (2000) won the Arts Council of Wales Book of the Year Award.

Kaite O'Reilly writes for theatre, radio and film, and works internationally as a dramaturge and tutor in performance writing. Her play *Yard* won the Peggy Ramsay Award. She is currently under commission to Sgript Cymru, Contact Theatre Manchester and Birmingham Rep. *peeling*, written for Graeae Theatre, was remounted and toured internationally in 2003/4. She is the recipient of the AHRB Creative Arts Fellowship at the University of Exeter 2003-2006 to further her own practice as a playwright/theatre practitioner.

Lloyd Robson, author of *cardiff cut* (Parthian), is a poet and prose writer whose texts work with typography, photography, visual art and performance. His most recent collection, *bbboing! and associated weirdness* (Parthian), was completed with the aid of an Arts Council of Wales writer's bursary.

John Williams lives and works in Cardiff. The author of five previous books, including the novels *Cardiff Dead* and *The Prince of Wales*, he also writes screenplays and freelance journalism. He is currently editing a collection of new Welsh fiction for Bloomsbury and working on his next book, which will include several pieces of short fiction and a novella. He is Chair of the Editorial Board of *New Welsh Review*.

Editorial Note:

Orthographical variants have been retained in order to preserve the individual visions of Cardiff collected in the book.

DOUBLE FOOTSTEPS

Dannie Abse

Our memories are card-indexed, consulted, and then put back in
disorder by authorities whom we do not control.

Cyril Connolly

1

The No. 2 platform at Cardiff Central Station was important and
busy with unsmiling soldiers heaving sausage-shaped white kit-
bags as I waited, lonesome, for the GWR train that would for some
four hours huff and puff and tamp along at 50 mph to Newport,
through the sulphur-loaded air of the Severn Tunnel, on to
Swindon, Reading and to my destination, the echoing, voluminous
Paddington Station. Sometimes it happened that the train hesitated
at the little platform of Baddington, allowing the huntin', shootin',
fishin', posh guests of the Duke of Beaufort to alight because of
contractual agreements signed privileged years ago by the GWR
board and the Duke.

My mother, whom I had managed to shoo away outside Cardiff
Station – 'Don't fuss, mother . . . Yes, I've got the Welsh cakes and
apples to eat on the train,' – was unhappy that I would be pursuing
my medical studies in blitzed London. After all, the previous year,
in February 1941, we had been bombed out of our house in
Windermere Avenue and I, a sixth-form schoolboy, had ended up,
brittle and baffled, in a small Cottage Hospital in Bridgend.
Besides, with my going away, the once loud house near Roath Park
Lake would be occupied only by my parents and the dog and
silence – my sister, Huldah, having left home years earlier, while
my eldest brother, Wilfred, called up into the Army, was encamped

somewhere in England, and Leo, too, who was in the RAF, had been posted to Bridlington.

That low-fahrenheit February evening in 1941 the air-raid hooter had sobered us up. We listened to its sorrowful moaning wail shredding the air. Soon we heard the serious, pulsating, arrhythmic drone of the German bomber planes and the answering lighter crackle and cough of the Ack-ack guns. The cacophony seemed more threatening than usual and the dog, as on other high decibel occasions, settled beneath the mahogany sideboard and blinked his brown, ponderous, enquiring eyes.

The previous Saturday morning at the Blackweir fields stretching behind Cardiff Castle, while playing rugby for my school, St Illtyd's College, I had been tackled with both my arms pinned as I fell on my right shoulder to the frosted unforgiving ground. I heard the sudden telltale click of my right clavicle snapping. Some of my team-mates, in their green and yellow hooped jerseys, their breath smoking, stood above me and one of them said, 'Swear if you like, mun.'

My mother and I, alert, hearing the war-rumble outside, sat uneasily in our living room – the black-out curtains against the windows, the wireless off, mute, the flickering and spitting coal fire in the grate, the dog, chin on his front paws, under the sideboard. 'I wish your father would come home,' my mother said, worried.

At last, when the front door opened, from the hall we heard him calling, 'Dannie, come outside. Good God, you've never seen anything like it.' We had experienced many raids before – once running home through the lane behind Windermere Avenue I had heard shrapnel crashing onto the dustbin lids outside the back doors – but as I stood with my father in the street, my arm in a sling because of my fractured collarbone, I realised this was something utterly different. It was the strange quality of an artificial light. No doubt, as usual above the barrage balloons, long fingering searchlights fumbled and probed the clouds and the stars above them but we were only aware of an intense green phosphorescent light – so bright that one could see every detail: the number on the front gate, a cigarette dibby in the gutter. As in some eerie dream the houses of Windermere Avenue cowered in the sickly green light and the road, too, pavements and all, had been painted a gangrenous green.

I shall never forget that green counterfeit light. We wondered at first what had spawned it. Green flares simply? We had heard about secret weapons. It crossed my mind: Could these be green death-rays?! 'Come in you two,' my mother called. 'Are you both mad?'

'They've mistaken Roath Park Lake for the Docks,' my father surmised. Mr Davies, our punctilious air-raid warden, appeared in his helmet, and together we then observed flares floating down slowly like snapped-off chandeliers – numerous small lights clustered around a big central flame, descending towards the green waters of Roath Park Lake.

'Incendiaries,' pronounced Mr Davies. 'Clusters of firebombs, the Molotov Bread Basket.'

Returned to the house, we took shelter in the little cloakroom below the staircase, and my father sensibly pinned up his heavy winter overcoat against the rear window to prevent lancing glass flying towards us should a bomb root itself close by. Just in time, too, for amongst the noise of aeroplanes and anti-aircraft guns we heard a distinct whine advancing, advancing, altering its note into a high-pitched whistle. The three of us were thrown across the hallway. The ceiling was down and a hole appeared in the wall through which we could witness again the gangrenous green light outside. I lay on the floor, my arm still in its sling, breathing in dust and plaster, and feeling the pain of the fractured collarbone.

'Are you all right? Are you all right?' my father called. Later we learned that Mr Davies, the ARP warden, had been killed.

But it wasn't because of the news about devastating air raids in London, or Lord Haw Haw on the wireless triumphantly telling us how the capital city of Britain would soon be razed to the ground, that made me disinclined to leave Cardiff. Cardiff was my home town, one that I felt attached to as if by an invisible umbilical cord.

Home town; well most admit an affection for a city:
grey tangled streets I cycled on to school, my first cigarette
in the back lane, and, fool, my first botched love affair.
First everything . . .

3

So many people I valued lived in Cardiff, so many occasions remembered, so many locations I cared for – why, only the day before leaving for London, I had lingered sentimentally at that small park across from Sandringham Road where I had once played for so long and so often. That park with its minnow-coloured stream, now devoid of surrounding railings – these taken away for the war effort – enclosed a foot-high waterfall. I would visit it as if it were a shrine whenever I experienced a boy's small failures or felt unaccountably melancholy. I thought its gentle rustling sound could console even a man condemned.

I would not have wished to depart from Cardiff and would not have done so had my name not been put down to study medicine years before at the Westminster Hospital Medical School. As the train pulled out from Platform 2 puffing steam from its unstitched sides, London, that city of strangers, seemed further than 150 miles away. Momentarily I knew the feeling Prince Boabdil must have experienced when exiled from his city. A mile away he looked back at the towers of the Alhambra and wept. Later I wrote a poem about leaving Cardiff which concluded:

For what *who* would choose to go
when *who* sailing had no choice?
Not for one second, I know,
can I be the same man twice.

The straw-coloured flames flare still,
spokes over the long horizon,
and the boats under the hill
of Penarth unload and move on.

2

Tentative and a little clumsy on the Westminster Hospital midwifery firm, I delivered babies who generally contrived to keep their appointments with this earth at 2 or 3 or 4 a.m. 'But you were born mid-afternoon,' my mother told me. 'Very convenient.'

That September afternoon in 1923 there was a typhoon in Japan following a Tokyo earthquake that left half a million dead. Years later at school I read how Glyndŵr claimed that 'the earth did shake when I was born.' Quite. Me and Glyndŵr! In Cardiff nature surely had been kinder, though it had probably been raining. It so often was. It so often is. That is why Cardiff is a city with grand sheltering arcades and why the grass in its numerous parks is so blatantly green.

I can imagine myself, a baby in a pram which my mother is guiding down the wet pavement of Whitchurch Road towards the house were I was born – No. 161, a plain grey, semi-detached, architecturally boring two-storied house. The rain, no doubt, is of the peculiarly Welsh variety, mistily damp, delicate, soft, almost colourless until, silvering, it hits the pavement. I can guess how the rain persistently arrived on the foliage of the dripping pavement and nested among the little leaves of the Whitchurch Road front garden hedges. Did I wonder what the noise was, that aggregate of rain put, put, putting, on the fabric of the pram's hood?

Soon after I was born my parents made the first of a number of rented house moves, initially to 289 Albany Road. I'm trying to remember that house and its surroundings. As Donald Davie once wrote, 'One remembers this or that; but to recollect it in the imagination so as to recreate it, then, ah, forced with that requirement the remembered past quite suddenly becomes drastically contracted.'

I remember, I remember, a certain tramstop in Newport Road opposite a long whitewashed wall. And as I inhabit a photograph of old Cardiff a tram appears. 'Not this one,' my mother says. How does she know it is not this one that will take us to my grandmother's house in Cowbridge Road? 'We want a 2A tram that goes to the Victoria Park terminus, not the No. 2 that ends up at the Pier Head in the Docks.' How does she know which is a No. 2A and not No. 2? An enigma. I do not yet recognise the figures on the seesawing yellow tramcars. Is it something to do with that pole touching sparks of light on the crackling wires above?

'Now, this is a No. 2A coming,' says my mother authoritatively.

My mother always sits downstairs. I decide she knows the destination of the tram because of the pattern in its golden-brown varnished downstairs ceiling. I noted how it was present in all the 2A tramcars. Indeed I can still summon that pattern to appear before my eyes as surely as William Blake could envisage the eidetic image of an angel or a flea. I close my eyes momentarily. Then and Now merge.

The tram stopped regularly along the Newport Road, passing the library where later I graduated from P. G. Wodehouse novels to more substantial works. Then it trundled past the Infirmary (where they kept babies for sale) and dipped beneath the bridge into Queen Street, stopping at the Capitol cinema; then on past the Kardomah to encounter, the other side of the road, the Castle with its filled moat.

So much has vanished, not least that moat, drained because it attracted too many insects. And the canal where during the Depression small boys dived for pennies, concreted over to become Churchill Way; the Dutch café bombed to smithereens during the war; the Empire Concert Hall (great ice creams) become a superstore; Queen Street itself pedestrianised; the corner house where my grandmother lived reconstructed into prose, into offices.

We moved again to 237 Albany Road. This new house seemed to attract more flies than No. 289. They circled the lampshade below the ceiling, the electric bulb their god, until giddy with their epiphany they landed and came to terminable grief on the hanging sticky flypaper.

Cardiff flies thrived because of the horses' trails of steaming khaki droppings – the smaller horses pulling the milk carts, rattling the glass bottles; the great twin cart horses dragging wagons heavy with piled up hundred-weights of coal; the four sleek black horses pulling a hearse to the graveyard. Observing a funeral procession people would halt and men would lift their caps or their trilbys or bowlers.

The flies also went to my school, Marlborough Road Elementary, another building that was bombed during the war. We were taught by, amongst others, Mr George Thomas, who later became an MP, subsequently the Speaker of the House of Commons ('Order, Order') and later still, Lord Tonypandy. He told us how Cardiff had become the greatest coal-exporting city in the world, how the Marquess of Bute built the docks and renovated the Castle.

'Does the present Marquess of Bute live in the Castle, Sir?'

'Sometimes, only sometimes, boy.'

One spring day, George Thomas took our class for an outing. We climbed the high Wenallt that allowed us a panoramic view of Cardiff. He pointed out to us the Castell Coch folly built by one of the Butes. '*Coch* is Welsh for red. So what do you think *Castell* means, Abse?'

Mr Thomas favoured me, probably because I was Jewish. That year, 1933, he must have known how the Nazi storm-troopers in Germany rapped on door after door to menacingly 'urge' the occupants to visit the local polling stations. Even those in the Dachau concentration camp were purported to have voted for the regime that had imprisoned them. Hitler received 90 per cent of all the votes.

I, a ten-year-old boy with Jewish parents, was fortunate that during the 1870s and 1880s my two grandfathers had emigrated to South Wales – the pious one to Ystalyfera in the Swansea Valley, the 'free thinker' to Bridgend. I, born in Cardiff, was lucky to have one Welsh-speaking grandfather, a scholar of the Old Testament, the Talmud and Jewish legends, anxious to pass on that heritage and the other who happily ignored the idolatry of all religions and who could not tell an *aleph* from a *beth*.

Before the war several hundred Jewish families lived in Cardiff, enough to people two congregations, one at a modest synagogue in Windsor Place, close to the Park Hotel, the other domed and gloriously prominent in Cathedral Road. (So many doctors practised in Cathedral Road it was called the Harley Street of Cardiff.) My mother, before my thirteenth birthday – after which I was allowed to choose a secular path – dispatched me on Saturday mornings to Windsor Place, but often I mitched in order to discover better entertainment in the National Museum. One evening a week, too, I had to attend the Windsor Place *cheder* where, with other pre-pubertal Cardiff Jewish boys, I was taught the Hebrew alphabet, the Old Testament stories and Midrashic fables by a Mr Moses Samuels, an eloquent Zionist and Talmudic scholar. Many years later I was able sometimes to call upon such biblical and Midrashic writings in the making of poems; most recently in 'Random Birthday Thoughts' where the Midrashic commentary adds to the biblical reference. The poem concludes:

And then I thought of how, when I was a boy,
I'd been told to use the word 'unique' rarely
since everything is; and of Abraham
ruining his father's business, wild
with an axe in the prosperous idol shop
screaming the Lord is One, the Lord is One.

In the drab basement room of the Windsor Place synagogue with
its map of Palestine on the wall, I listened to such biblical stories
and fanciful extensions of them – Mr Samuels being as fervent as
St David who, it is said, sometimes stood up to his neck in the cold
water of a lake reciting scriptures.

But the Abse family hardly accepted the disciplined structures,
celebrations and schedules of Jewish life. True, my mother would
light two candles every Friday night, offer a silent prayer with her
hands before her shut eyes and then regale us with a kosher meal
from a butcher's shop in Bridge Street. My atheist father, tolerant
of all this, occasionally played snooker in the Jewish Club that was
situated before the war above two shops in St Mary's Street. Both,
whom I loved dearly, now lie in their chemistry in the small Jewish
cemetery near Roath Park Lake.

3

Last Saturday morning you could have discovered me at
Paddington collecting *The Guardian* and *The Western Mail* from
W. H. Smith – necessary reading matter over the next two hours'
journey to Cardiff. I intended to visit Ninian Park to watch the
Bluebirds play Wycombe Wanderers. I managed to settle myself in
a window seat before being joined by a bespectacled, suit-and-tie
young man who promptly extracted a mobile phone from his
pocket. Ignoring him, I tried to concentrate on the Sports page of
The Western Mail.

At present the Bluebirds still play at Ninian Park, which pitch
once served as Cardiff Corporation's rubbish tip. But the
Grandstand season ticket holder seated several rows behind me
regularly and urgently cries out, 'Fuckin' rubbish,' referring to the

opposing team rather than to any geographical source. Ninian Park's stadium itself has shrunk – the lofty pre-war Canton and Grangetown sloping stands have been bisected to accommodate a mere 20,000 spectators. In the sepia Saturday afternoons 60,000 Woodbine-smoking, swaying fans used to cheer on Cardiff City FC and abuse the Ref.

The tidy young man sitting next to me in carriage D continued to address his mobile all the way to Reading. I could not help hearing his staccato conversation about some terrific business contract that would be in jeopardy unless his auditor took his sober advice. It seemed some guy called Francis (or was it a woman called Frances?) had mucked up the whole thing so that my phone-mad travelling companion had to unbraid the convoluted situation by scheme (a) or (b) or (c) or . . . The train was packed else I would have considered moving. I recollected how Cecil Day Lewis, on a train journey, was recognised by a ticket collector who insisted the Poet Laureate be upgraded to a First Class carriage.

I, too, have had one such triumph – in Cardiff twenty years ago. I'd been for a walk round Roath Park Lake, but ten minutes after leaving the park I experienced a dire need to pee. I was then walking near the Eastern end of Ninian Road close to the Rec, where, as a wanton schoolboy, I played football or Welsh baseball and I recalled that, at the Western side of the Rec there used to be a public urinal. My diuretic anxieties increased when I reached my destination: the public lavatory now, astonishingly, served women only! Fortunately I espied a public library nearby, housed in a pre-fabricated, temporary-looking building.

Inside a man was seriously stamping books. 'Have you a loo here?' I inquired quietly. He raised his head slowly, lowered his head slowly then resumed his stamping routine. At last he replied, 'Not for the public. Only for the staff and desperate poets!' There you are: Cardiff is no longer a philistine city. There's Chapter Arts Centre; St David's Hall; the Sherman Theatre; the Welsh Opera Company; the Museums at Park Place and St Fagan's; the Bay; the pedestrian streets; bookshops that contain one or two real books; and librarians with urological sympathy for poets.

As the train drew into Cardiff Central Station I wondered how many of the luggage-collecting passengers were visiting my home

9

town for the first time. They would be immediately startled by the assertive white masts and the Speer-like gigantism of the Millennium Stadium that had been born from the conjugation of beneficent, fertilising lottery money and the perennial Welsh addiction to Rugby.

I'm not sure how I feel about it. Sometimes I admire its brazen suggestion of a large ship, grounded appropriately close to the River Taff; other times I resent the bullying way it dominates the surrounding area, insistently commanding, 'Look at me. Look at me.'

I know what Lloyd Wilbur Junior would have thought of the Millennium Stadium. Some years ago my cousin Derek, detailed to meet that cigar-chewing Texan businessman at Cardiff Station, decided to show him something of Wales's capital city. The Texan arrived wearing a cowboy hat, with his mouth precisely fitted to a large cigar.

'Mr Lloyd Wilbur?' asked Derek, who had not met him before.

'Yeah. How didja know?'

Confronted by Derek's Mini Minor, Junior laughed. 'What's this?' he queried. 'A car? My Gawd, it's dinky. A car! You got somethin' to sell there, boy.'

After a few minutes' drive up Westgate Street, suddenly Lloyd Wilbur screamed, 'Stop the car!' My cousin, alarmed, brought the car to an emergency stop.

'What's that?' boomed the Texan, pointing his finger Northwards.

'The Castle,' Derek almost whispered. 'Cardiff Castle.'

'A castle. My Gawd, a castle in the middle of a town. That's darlin'. You've got somethin' to sell there, boy.'

At Roath Park again the imperious command: 'Stop . . . the . . . car.'

'This is a lake. You're tellin' me this pond is a lake. Gawd. An' what's that?'

'It's a lighthouse, a memorial for Captain Scott,' explained Derek. 'You see Captain Scott –'

'Oh my Gawd,' interrupted Lloyd Wilbur Junior. He became Laughter holding both his sides. 'A lighthouse . . . ha ha ha . . . a lighthouse for rowing boats. You certainly got somethin' to sell there, boy.'

Yes, I know what Junior would have said about the Millennium Stadium – the same words he would have said on encountering the Pyramids of Egypt, the ruined Greek temples of Paestum, the Roman aqueducts, or the great Gothic cathedrals – 'You've got somethin' to . . .'

Coming out of Cardiff station I was assaulted, as in the past, by the sight of a particularly ugly slab of modern sculpture, not redeemed by carrying lines from verses by Cardiffian poets including some of my own:

No sooner than I'd arrived the other Cardiff had gone,
smoke in the memory, these but tinned resemblances,
where the boy I was not and the man I am not
met, hesitated, left double footsteps, then walked on.

Soon I was walking on, boy and man, to pass the building that was once the Prince of Wales Theatre. I saw my first play there on a school trip – *The Merchant of Venice*. I was impressed by how far Donald Wolfit, impersonating Shylock, could spit.

Across the road in St Mary's Street I entered the bedlam of memories.

Suddenly it was 1974, when the first part of my autobiography, *A Poet in the Family*, had been published but was not for sale in Lears Bookshop. The sales director of Hutchinson told me that the old purse-lipped proprietor had ordered 50 copies but had cancelled them when he happened on a page where I described my meeting with swearing Nina Hamnett, the painter from Tenby who had once been a model for Modigliani and Epstein.

Lears bookshop no longer survives, unlike the nearby Louis' Restaurant where I decided to have lunch. The restaurant had not altered at all. The same menu. The same waitresses, grown older of course. I reminded myself how Kierkegaard had recommended that life must be lived forwards but can only be understood backwards. So, after lunch, I continued my forward and backward journey and reached Cowbridge Road where Ivor Novello's profile once lived, and where, a few doors away, my Uncle Max had had his medical practice. There, soon after qualifying, I once worked

11

as his locum when he went on holiday. I recall how I shook in my shoes even more than my patients did.

Ahead of me I could see the defunct, empty St David's Hospital where I had visited a different uncle of mine who was recovering from pneumonia. I was not welcome; his secret mistress was in attendance. Now I looked up at the high clock on its tower. It had stopped at ten to two – in the early morning I suspect, in the darkness, 'the time of night when Troy was set on fire, the time when screech-owls cry and barn dogs howl', and the time when some patients in St David's died. This was not Grantchester.

Cardiff has changed for the better, but as I walked on, in indigo mood, I could only think of inestimable people and places that have vanished: the Globe Cinema in Roath, where on Saturday mornings for fourpence I could sit in the posh balcony and hurray the cowboy, Buck Jones, and weep for the dog, Rin Tin Tin; the red-leathered Kardomah café in Queen Street where I had boiling arguments with friends about whether Evolution or Revolution was best; the tennis courts in Waterloo Gardens where I would play with Boris who, too often, shouted 'Out' and who collected absurd lines from current films: *So long Toulouse; Natch, Gloria, natch; Don't crowd me, you bum; Here's lookin' at you, kid.*

All gone like those girlfriends of the kissing lanes. And gone, too, literary friends such as Aled Vaughan, John Ormond and John Tripp. Dead, dead, dead, as Dylan Thomas would have recited plummily. I glanced at my wristwatch. Soon the game at Ninian Park would begin. I walked beside the Ninian pub and passed under the two shabby, leaking railway bridges. In Sloper Road all the people, anonymous people, walked in the same direction, I among them, and as a cloud turned the October sun to shade, I felt I was inhabited by my own ghost.

CARDIFF – THE CITY THAT FLOATS

Peter Finch

Before the city, where did the waters reach? Most everywhere. Cairdife on its slump of pudding-stone. Cardiff bounded by moor, salt marsh, alluvial tide field, estuary and sinking mud. Before the sea walls were raised, the spring tides brought salt water as far as the bottom of St Mary Street and drowned the car parks of MFI and Castle Bingo along Newport Road. This was a pond, this place. Water in runs and ditches. And the wind bringing in rain, as it still does, in dark enveloping clouds from the Atlantic, from the southwest. I'm in Mount Stuart Square, solid Victorian, once home of shipping companies, coal traders and merchant banks. Over the past one hundred and fifty years, as Cardiff slowly moved from industrial powerhouse to postmodern mall, the Square and its occupants have changed. Gone is nineteenth-century commerce. Gone too twentieth-century grit, dabble and decline. In their place are twenty-first century liberal arts – broadcasters, blond-floored apartments, bars, media companies. At their centre the monolithic Coal Exchange, once vibrant with top-hatted traders selling options in not-yet-cut Aberdare steam coal, and now home to concerts by Captain Paranoid and the Delusions, Jefferson Starship, Van Morrison and Otis Grand.

Before Bute built his great docks, and well before the Exchange was built in 1884, this patch of land was little more than a sandbank, ringed with high-tide driftwood, and housing Guest's Glass Works. Bottles, cups, jars. Window glass for the Empire well-to-do and the expanding American market. The smoking towers were used by incoming vessels as a beacon. The pits Guest had dug went nine metres down into sticky clay subsoil before they hit anything solid.

13

Butetown was Soudrey – Sowdrie, Southrew, Sawdry, Sutton – the South Town. Orthography was imperfect: you spelled the place as you thought it sounded. There were saw mills and a sea-washed track running from the sea to the town's South Gate. You could fish. Pollution hadn't begun. The tides were full of great white horses. The moorland was ponded and thick with reed grass. The Taff, meandering without restraint, held fishing henges and beaten-earth slipways from which coracles were launched. This was a tiny place. If you lived here you weren't much. If you were anything you didn't come here at all.

I'm walking where the dry route used to be: Bute Street, known first as Bute Road down here and as Lewis Street at its northernmost extremity. It's littered with well-meaning street art and traffic-calming chicanes. Where the paving slopes buggy-friendly towards the tarmac, locals have beached their Vauxhalls. The shrub plantings beyond the railway station are full of blown plastic and crushed lager cans. My plan is to follow where the hard earth used to be until I reach the dry land of Rumney Hill to the east. I'm ley walking. Leys are straight tracks channelling power from ancient site to ancient site. They network the globe. Where they intersect there's sway and magic. The cosmic power they carry keeps the planet alive. Alfred Watkins discovered these alignments in 1921 and wrote up his theories in *The Old Straight Track*. Welsh feng shui. The ancient routes of Celtic power. But in the city they get lost. Where they encounter industrial hard-core, excavation, canal, culverted river and other man-made despoliation, the leys alter. Their energy blackens, becomes dissipated. They bend, they sink. Buggered leys broken across the Dumballs. St Mary's to the sunken iron-age sea harbour, no longer visible. St John's to the Great Reen, sunk. The Longcross to the Ely's tidal limits, twisted beyond recognition. But I'm going back to a time before this despoliation. I'm tracking where they used to flow.

Along Mermaid Quay the Faber novelist and museum director, J. O. Jones, once celebrated his love of writing by arranging for the now demolished Maritime Museum to host poetry readings. The late John Ormond, film-maker and Oxford poet, read his 'Renoir Blue' in the main gallery here. Blue water, blue slate, blue graves, blue lazulite, blue slipper-clay, blue anything, blue everything, blue everywhere. John Tripp, heart on sleeve, full of Big Windsor beer, stomped and heckled. Trouble with you, Ormond, he said, you don't engage with the people. What do they know about lazulite Renoir? What do they care? The crowd, no one local, all imports from the city two miles north, stood in edgy silence. What next? Would the poet flatten his swaying critic? Ormond coughed, looked about, held his hand characteristically to his bad ear, straining to listen, heard, acted as if he had not. The poems continued. Tripp gave up. Through the museum's great windows the mud-flatted Bay whirled with birds. Afterwards, back at Ormond's house in Pontcanna, Tripp would take a swing at the poet B. S. Johnson, miss, collapse across the coffee table and have to be made to leave. We're still the best of friends, he told me later, me and Ormond, we understand each other, this is how it is. Ah yes.

The world rarely changes in essence. Today, in the Ship and Pilot, Darren, or someone with a name like that, tells me he's not out to waste his useful time talking to muppets. He knows I'm not from round here. This is a small community. Everyone knows everyone else. I'm from Lisvane. No. Well, you're from th'apaartmunts, then, you should be drinkin in Bar38. Norere. This aint the Bay. It is not. I buy him a drink, no use falling out over nothing, dangerous in deep Butetown, whatever the night. He has a double Southern Comfort and Coke. I don't take my notepad out. The Bay is two communities existing in the same space-time continuum. They pass through each other as they move. They rarely interact.

Heading north I skirt the Oval Basin, once the sea entrance to the Bute East Dock and later home to *The Sea Alarm*, preserved museum relic, cut for scrap in 1999 by three men with thermal lances working behind screens so that the innocent, protesting public would not see. The original plan was to rebuild the Maritime Museum elsewhere and keep the collection intact. Where? No one was sure. While we waited, the treasures would be stored in rail sidings at Treforest. They would be put in packing cases in rented warehouses. They would be stored in converted bomb-storage tunnels at the Royal Navy Armaments Depot, Trecŵn. They'd be sent to the moon. They'd be okay. They are the

15

cream of Wales's now fast reducing industrial heritage. Sourced and restored at great cost. Some scrapyard in Newport got the remains of *The Sea Alarm*. I've no idea who got the rest.

The Basin, renamed The Roald Dahl Plass after the local, scowling author, is now decked with slatted hardwood and open for public use as a playground. You get food fairs here, tented exhibitions of prime Welsh beef burgers, Caws Llangloffan Cheese, Llannerch Cariad Dry White Wine, Rice Pudding from Llangadog, clog dancers for authenticity. As I pass, the place is full of rally cars, the sun bounding off their over-waxed surfaces, photographers nuzzling them like hungry sheep.

On the west side of the Basin stands Stefan Gec's *Deep Navigation*. Using bollards from the dock and disused rail from Tower Colliery, the sculptor has cast two steel pillars at just over human scale. The rusting sculptures, which resemble pit-props, have brass plates affixed to them. They bear the names of the ports to which coal had once been shipped from the West Bute and the names of the South Wales pits from which the black gold came. Not that you need this information to appreciate the work. It explains itself.

I turn left here, skirt the snub-end of the filled-in West Dock, Bute's first, now covered with pale brick apartments bearing Italianate seafaring names. The docks were what made Cardiff. Before they came, the population was less than 2000. Now they've gone we approach 350,000. We came here and we flourished in the service of the docks and the materials they carried – iron, steel, coal. They're gone but signs of their former power are still around. It's in the shape of the roadways. It's in the soil below the paving. It's among the dock impedimenta – the bollards, anchor links, and steam-shovel jaws – which are fixed along the walkways like so many fairy lights. The ley is sunk but flowing. I track it up.

Rather than walk through new housing, I cross instead to the Bute East Dock. It's still in place, full of water, but with its access to the sea blocked. It's still serviced by the canal-like Bute Dock Feeder. This was dug in the early nineteenth century to bring water down from Blackweir on the Taff to stop the Docks silting up. The Bute East is empty: two swans, a slick of oil at the top end (dumped there by some local car-fixer who couldn't be arsed), *The*

Ebden Hazler, the last barge on the water, roped as a bit of décor to the edge of Brain's new-build family pub, The Wharf. This dock once shifted ships like NCP processes cars. Forty-two acres of water servicing 1200 vessels annually. The stats we want to hear. It's leisure now. Chinese dragon races, a bit of power-boating, much fishing. The quay is lined with signs giving stern warnings against toxicity and algae which will bite into your face like an alien. Do not enter these waters. The fisherman I pass, tented and sat here for six hours already, has caught nothing, might soon, doesn't care. They're protecting themselves with those notices, he tells me. They always do. He's not concerned. We look out across the grey-green water. A gull lands like Concorde on floats. Diving ducks scour the grubby bottom. There's a Sunny Delight bottle and a stack of burger casings. Some scaffold poles. A bike wheel. But mostly clear.

As a child this part of the Docks always frightened me. Huge water discovered suddenly in the heart of the built-up city, or so it seemed. I'm trying now to put it in place, make something from it, fit it into the internal urban landscape I'm creating. Turning what's in front of your eyes into something that can be written down isn't easy. Do what Joyce did. Put the whole day down as one. Interior, exterior, first thoughts, best thoughts, all of them crammed onto the valid page? Go with Glyn Jones' contention that, if you let it, the one idea you have will just roll like a snowball, gathering other things to itself, growing rapidly until it's either topsy or done? Or be like considered Sebald or demented Sinclair, walking with your notepad, letting your mind go off in whatever direction it chooses? Painters have it so much easier: daub, line, scratch, done. Somewhere in the contemporary surface around me, or just under it where I can still reach if I stretch, is the real city. A shimmer of the past, still there in the ether, just, in the whorls of dust, in the way the earth has settled, in the dried surface marks and in the etchings of rust. Catch it, touch it, hold it. Be quick before the mind moves. Fickle. On.

Bute, the second Marquess, John Crichton Stuart, the man whose wealth and vision built Cardiff, only ever came here when he had to. His ghost, serge-suited, creases hot-ironed by his manservant, walks in front, gazes though thick eye-glasses across the blank water. Cardiff, so damp. He ran his empire by correspondence from his family seat, Mount Stuart, on the Isle of Bute. Dour and distant, afflicted with poor vision, ruthless, tireless. He bullied his estate managers and his agents into a precision of action of which Bill Gates would have been proud. It was he, more than his Catholic, romantic and utterly fantasist son, the third Marquess, who drew the marks on the map that turned Cardiff from slumbering backwater into exploding industrial force. By the mid-nineteenth century the town had become the world's largest coal-exporter. Forty years, that's all it took. Like Gates, Bute owned the entire operating system. There were no rivals to speak of. When one rose (such as Davies the Ocean's docks at Barry), Bute simply improved his own operation. Put in a new rail access. Dug a new basin. Built a new wharf. He was irresistible. He owned everything. Early Cardiff maps, with the Bute lands on them coloured red, look like the world at the height of the British Empire. Bute, Celtic highlander, protestant, builder. A foreign founder. But now a fading ghost, a wraith of mist along the wind-blown water. His names and those of his descendants permeate the city. Bute Park. The Bute Dock public house. Bute Crescent. Bute Street. Bute Road. But who was he? Who were his powerful family? Today, hardly anyone knows.

Along Lloyd George Avenue the warehouses have all been pulled down. The one that remains is being turned into the Granary flats. Enveloped. Nineteenth-century stone carcass, twenty-first century interior. The sign outside says *More Than Just Apartments*. But someone last week spray-painted the *Just* and added a *No*. It read *No More Than Apartments*. Got it. The graffiti was removed within days.

My ley pushes itself through the top of the dock and into the space where St Paul's once stood. This was the religious heart of vanished Newtown, little Ireland, home of half of Bute's workers for 150 years, bulldozed in a fit of self-righteous corporate slum clearance in the nineteen-sixties. Here Bay turns to Adamsdown turns to Splott. Legendary working-class districts. Hotbeds. Road-calmed. Full of pubs and people on the street. Unvisited real Cardiff. Unless you happen to live here, of course.

The Black Bridge and Beyond

Adamsdown, which I enter by the Black Bridge across the main rail line, took its name from Adam Kyngot, who in 1331 was sometime porter at Cardiff Castle and who farmed here. 'A large piece of land – a messuage in the Parish of Roath' John Hobson Matthews calls Adamsdown in his Victorian *Cardiff Records*. A messuage is a piece of land on which a dwelling-house is erected, and they've put up a few of those. Little sign of Kyngot now. This territory is covered with rebuilt workers' housing, rail sidings and drinking clubs. The Black Bridge is one of the oldest in the city, built in 1850, the same time as the Broad Gauge rail line arrived here from Gloucester. It's a mess of black iron-girders and massive bolts filled in with bitumen-painted corrugated sheet. It's supposed to be pockmarked with German machine-gun shells from 1943, but among the rust and rivets of time I've never found any. The bridge rises from the newly built but rarely open Sanquhar Street temple to drop into Kames Street, Pertuce Ltd, green-shuttered, windows barred, *loans arranged*, the Adamsdown Gospel Hall and a sprawl of urban paint spray that goes back thirty years.

In the eighties, the Adamsdown Writers established themselves here. This was an overtly and unabashed working-class republic of letters. The democratisation of the form was paramount. Members would move out from their garrets to create a genuine writers' co-operative. The politics of the group's actions were as important as their actual literary output. They set themselves tasks: write a paper on what you think we mean by 'working-class culture'; discuss how established cultural institutions are one-way conveyor belts for ruling class ideology; why is the cultural struggle not a safe struggle? Adamsdown Writers' activities were powered by alcohol rather than dope. They needed that engaging steam. A drug-hazed floating mind usually leads to no more than beatific smiles.

In order to draw the attention of the public to their aim of disestablishing literature, the group, dressed mainly in airware and flighties, took over a section of the recently pedestrianised Queen Street in the city centre. They affixed to its surface the text of poems which proved their point. *Change the past. Do it now. We are Albion. We are Blake reborn.* They handed out the same texts mimeographed up as A5 flyers. They sat down. Completely ignorant of the country in which they operated, or possibly not caring, they acted as they thought writers might have done when the Winter Palace was stormed. Strong. Supporters of the workers. Resolute.

I watched all this from my city-centre bookshop – I was running the Charles Street Oriel at the time and felt I'd done my years as an activist. Faced down the capitalists. Stood against the monoglots. Been out there in the street selling verse, read it aloud to drinkers in pubs who didn't want to know, stood on platforms, handed it out as leaflets, free. There's only so much you can put up with. There's only so much that outrage can do. My stuff was now sealed inside books that you could only unlock if you bothered to find them. Vision. History. Ecstasy. Process. Art. These streetwise littérateurs were into direct action, confrontation, opposition; poetry that went well beyond its constituent words.

The workers' reaction to the Adamsdown performance was, as might have been expected, mute. *The South Wales Echo* ran a report about New Romantics and how poetry was once again on target in its world game of moving itself closer to the people. If you paid any attention to the press you'd think that poetry had been steadfastly doing this for the past fifty years. The people remained unmoved. Back in Adamsdown the writers drank from cans outside the Great Eastern. It was summer. The light came in shafts through the plane trees, warmed the dust of the streets. Thatcher was at the helm and poll tax was looming. Poetry makes nothing happen, said Auden. Could he have been right? Soon Militant would galvanise the local population into a red wedge of disobedience. Can't Pay Won't Pay. Fight the Tax. No Poll Tax Here. The slogans would adorn the Black Bridge, the walls of pedestrian underpasses, and every phone relay box from here to Canton. The battle had a vigour and engagement which their poetry somehow could not touch. Who wanted alien distant Blake when a real battle like this was within grasp? The poets changed texts for diatribe and their pens for spray cans.

Turning right just before the Great Eastern, I track along backstreets full of speed humps and front doors which open directly onto them. Splott's Edwardian workers' housing might have been much better than Newtown's insanitary back-to-backs, but it still lacked space. Road grit lines the window edges. Old newspapers blow along the paving. At the back of Clifton Street the frozen chicken warehouse has I LOVE YOUR MUM'S TITS scratched into the paint of its anonymous doors. This is one of the council's inner-city bikeways. Blue signs on poles. Marked pathways. No one on them but cars and dogs.

This is also Lloyd Robson territory. A post-Poll Tax scribbler with a neo-Dadaist hatred of capital letters, he has now made Cardiff poetry very much his own. 'yu nose ow splott sounds bad ri? so we'r told any road, cos it' sounds liek SPOT or SPLATT!' Ask some of the swoony women who want to mother him after one of his stuttery performances at Chapter. Robson has eclipsed his rivals. Streetwise, football-mad, articulate. His *cardiff cut*, billed as a novel but more like a long poem, tells the whole tale and has earned him a real legitimacy. The heavy streets. The hard streets. The hooligan streets. Not those of the past but the ones alive right now. Robson spends much of his time photographing the road signs and obtuse graffiti of these streets and nearby City Road. His montages are worth any amount of classic reportage. Explorations of *how* we are in these gritty places and the ways in which we change: that is his territory. Edge Territory. Look him up. It's around 11.00 a.m. as I cut through Diamond Street, along Cecil Street and onto Broadway. Robson doesn't do mornings. I don't knock on his door.

Roath

We're in Roath now, the classic workers' town. Meshed terraces spread east from the industrial city. Roath originally stretched the whole way from the Crockerton East Gate to the Rumney River. Rath. Raz. The name has a hard, pre-British sound. There's a theory which I like enormously that the city should never have been called Cardiff in the first place. Its original name was Roath. Ptolemy, the early Egyptian warlord and geographer who compiled the first world maps from the gossip of itinerant mariners, has a place called Ratostathibios scratched in on the papyrus, next to the

Taff, more or less where Cardiff Castle came to stand. Say that word a few times. You can make it sound like Roath. Like Taff. Râth-Tâv. Y Rhâth. Roath on the Taff taking in everything from the Ely to the Rumney. When the country came to be divided into parishes, Cardiff, by then already a burgh, became the name for the western half and Roath for the east. The division was a matter of administrative convenience, no more than that. Cardiff, with its Castle, its quay and its navigable river grew in importance. Roath, with its hillfort-sited church, mill and manor house, remained a village. Until the nineteenth century, that is, when Bute's industrial expansion filled the fields between the two places with tenements and streets. Roath, capital of Wales. Could have been.

Where Roath begins and ends today is a subject of dispute. Parts of its southern extremity have been taken over by Adamsdown, Splott, Atlantic Wharf, Tremorfa and Pengam. To the north Cathays, Penylan, Waterloo and Plasnewydd all encroach. I've always lived in Roath. When I was a child we seemed to move every couple of years as part of some financial management scheme of my father's. He theorised that if you bought and sold judiciously you could make enough spare to get by on. Not that his schemes ever appeared to actually generate much cash. We went from Kimberley Road to Waterloo Gardens to Tŷ Draw Place to Westville Road. Always Cardiff east, which my mother insisted that I either call Penylan or Roath Park, depending on which house we happened to be in at the time. It was the same for our brief sojourn in Canton. When we were there I had to put Victoria Park down as the district. In later life she actually did move to Penylan, although her letters then labelled the place as Lakeside. God knows what would have happened if she'd made it to Lisvane. She probably wouldn't have regarded that as Cardiff at all.

The main highway east, when I get to it, is Newport Road. This link passes on through the site of the Roath Court manor house's gatehouse; past Cardiff's best unreconstructed Brains pub, The Royal Oak, with its second-floor boxing gym, its rock music back room and its heavy-booted regulars, and out onto what was once the causeway. The flatland between here and the eastern rise of Rumney Hill was (and still is if you peer between the tarmac) bogland. These are the great eastern salt marshes which, before the building of the sea wall, were regularly inundated at high tide. Here was an almost East Anglian landscape of reed, fishing henge and drainage gully. Salmon. Shrimp. Crab. Grass. Bladderwrack. Today it's shopping mall territory. Supermarkets, drive-in burger bars, carpet warehouses, office supplies, curtains, pots with fish painted on their sides, fitted kitchens, basket-weave dining suites, emulsion paint, wooden garden ornaments, drill bits that cost £1 a dozen but snap as soon as you put them anywhere near a wall. Newport Road blazes out along the line of the ancient Portway, the Roman road that ran from Isca to Nidum, Caerleon to Neath. It's been here a while, this route.

To the south, the streets of Splott and Tremorfa are hampered by a dense corrugation of speed humps that slow even the Kawasakis that leap across them. Road deaths in poorer districts were long thought to be the fault of addled youth spinning sparks out of the road surface in their side-skirted, sewer-piped Peugeots and speaker-stuffed Novas. Research has shown that they are more a product of the amount of time people here actually spend on the streets and the number they need to cross in order to get where they are going. Still, nothing quite like seeing a gleaming boy racer fingering his earring as he boomboxes along at a five mph crawl. On the causeway it's a different matter. Six lanes of solid diesel doing fifty make the proposition of walking to get anywhere terminally daunting. America has landed. You don't like this Berber twist? Drive next door to see what theirs is like.

I walk it anyway, sidestepping through low parking-bay walls and between the massed transport of south Wales' afternoon shoppers. The flat I used to rent in the last south-side terrace block of Edwardian three-stories has now been refashioned as Dijabrindab Eerwidja, an Asian grand residence next to where the brickworks used to be. I began my writing career here. Tried it as a singer with a guitar, harmonica harness, bottle caps on my shoes, the whole bit. I did out-of-tune, self-penned folk songs. Drizzle-drenched Bob Dylan. South Wales Donovan. I was terrible. I toured the pubs. This is what folk singers did, I'd heard. Got in the bar, scraped, clanged. I got thrown out of everywhere. Even the scrumpy drunks in the Greyhound couldn't cope. Cun you do Nelliedean? Well sodoffthen. So I went back to the flat and turned my awful songs into awful poems. Time improved them. I think. I wrote 'Welsh Wordscape' there, pissed off with Wales' self-referential tie-wearing conservatism. Where was the future? Somewhere else.

Rumney

I approach the foot of Rumney Hill, on the far side of the Rumney River, in what was once Monmouth. Here stands the Grade II listed Rumney Pottery. My rusty ley runs straight at it. The building, right on the edge of the river with the remains of an ancient riverside quay outside, looks much like any middle-class suburban semi. White pebble-dash, cotoneaster over the door, gravel drive. Records show this place to have been making pots for at least five hundred years, four hundred of them by the same family.

The present potter, Robert Giles, tells me he was probably the one who was here making tea sets when I visited on a school trip in the sixties. He's not in awe of history. His family of craftsmen goes back at least eight generations on this site. He shows me the kiln, scratching clay as he speaks. The workshop is full of unfinished ceramic work, wooden bench, pots stacked on slatted shelves, dust. Through the window I can see where the horse-powered pug mill which churned the dug clay once stood. He tells me he used to dig the clay himself, from just across the river where Magnet Joinery now stands. Gave it up. Didn't seem right excavating six-foot holes in real estate which belonged to someone else. Where does the clay come from today? Some English China from Cornwall, but mostly it's shipped in from Brazil. The pottery was famous in the nineteenth century for its domestic water pitchers and bread crocks, and later for its Victorian wash sets and utilitarian washing pans widely used in the mining valleys. Today, work is virtually all done on commission. Sgraffito slipware for schools, churches, golf clubs. Mugs with your name on them. Plates with a society badge at their centre. In production during my visit is a commemorative plate for the International Association of Practice Accountants. Big dinner coming up in Cardiff. All attending guests will get one in a decorative box to take home. The Pottery bestseller is a four-inch *skulldish* made to a special design for

Welsh band the Super Furry Animals. Can I buy one? No, you'll have to talk to them about that. It might be old, but the Rumney Pottery stays up to date. Has its own web presence, makes enough of a living to keep a family, welcomes visitors, doesn't pressure them to buy too much. The grey river slides past us outside. Its mud glistens.

Across the bridge I leave the city. Or rather pass where the city once finished. Before 1938, the village of Rumney and what's now greater Cardiff east of the river either didn't exist or were not administered from City Hall. Here on the hillside my map shows an ancient monument – Rumney Castle, *Cae Castell*. The map is a nineteen-eighties OS, surveyed before the great Bay development began. But ancient monuments don't disappear, do they? According to the records this was one of the Welsh-subduing fortifications built on Roman foundations by Robert Fitzhamon, the eleventh-century Norman Lord of Glamorgan. An obvious target for a ley. Looking now for its remains is not a simple matter. The site, I discover, was formally excavated in 1978. Coins and pottery were found, wall footings photographed, Norman ringworks were traced. All on land reported as 'behind the Oaklands Hotel'. The collected evidence was deposited at the headquarters of the Glamorgan Gwent Archaeological Trust. In 1983 this building then burned down. All that remain now are memories. And ash. The Oaklands has been renamed Sizzlers. The Rumney Castle site has been flattened by the building of houses along the new Castle Avenue and Crescent. What is there left to see? Behind the bar no one knows. As I leave I am followed into the car park by two entirely pissed women, handbags whirling around them, clinging to each other's coats for balance. This is Sunday afternoon. They've been out for lunch and done two bottles of Sizzlers' red each. It's here, slurs one, gesticulating. Her arm waves in the general direction of a rubbish-strewn slope. I climb through the fence and look out over the snaking river and damp paddock below. Not a brick or carved stone block to be seen. When Rumney Castle fell out of use as a defensive structure in around 1270, it was turned into a manor house and home for the Norman Gilbert de Clare's mother, the Countess Maud. Noble blood. You'd think something would be left to mark the fact. All I can see are weeds. The staggerers reach their battered Maxi, giggling, dropping their keys in the gravel. You shouldn't get into that, I tell them. I can see snow out there on the hills in the distance, way beyond the city. Why not, they shout. They both sprawl into the rear seat and leave the vehicle driverless. Better than going home.

Edge and On

At the back of Rumney Hill Gardens, a small well-manicured collection of tennis courts and bowling greens reminiscent of a retired seaside town, there's a bridle path leading off the hill into the valley beneath. Negotiating it is a bit of a stumble through woodland and bramble. But it's passable. It leads to a reed-strewn, flat-bottomed valley running northeast away from the city. It looks much like Cardiff must have done millennia ago. Green. Quiet. In the far distance I can see a rugby game and some low changing rooms. There are a few pylons bringing the city power but they don't dominate. On the hillsides themselves are the great networks of orange brick estate – to the south vast Llanrumney, and the north, above the Eastern Avenue road link, Llanedeyrn and Pentwyn. But the valley itself stays largely empty.

The path through the reed beds heads for the Rumney, and then follows it on out and far away from the diesel and grit of the stainless-steel capital. Through the trees on the water's north side I spot a ten-year-old on a Honda Fireblade track bike. The earth heaps I can see along the trail I'm following are not the unfinished remains of construction but rural speed humps. There's a burned-out car slumped in a creek. A traffic cone in the bushes. Some hard core strewn among the willows. But for a place this close to huge inhabitation it's still not much. Human intervention is minimal. The silence comes in like a cloud. Water, soft sound of the river. The places it passes now are nearly all pre-industrial – Church Farm, Bridge Farm, White Barn, Tai Derwen, Tŷ Hir Farm, Minorca, Gwern Leyshon Wood, Coed Craig Ruperra, Draethen. The Rumney snakes and turns. The Welshness of the landscape re-asserts itself. The ground slowly swells. The ley is back. I can feel it. Power, history, strength. But Cardiff – city and capital – that's gone.

CF11: CARDIFF IN SIX FUGUES, 1992–2001*

Kaite O'Reilly

i

She died in the house she was born in. A terraced three up three down, with stairs hidden in a cupboard. It had an unusually spacious middle room for such a small house, but that was courtesy of the progressive joiners who built it as a model artisan dwelling for their workers. There was a yard, with outside WC and a coal shed, the bags for which had to be carried through the whole house, leaving a trail of dust on the black and ochre quarry slate tiles. Out back there was ten feet of scrubbed paving-stones before the joiners' wall. The wall was uneven, made of stones and rocks from over twenty-six countries, counterweight from the belly of foreign boats, brought from faraway lands and dumped onto the dockside, later carted away and turned into hotels and schools and workplaces and public houses.

The uneven stone wall rose up high, blocking out the sun. She didn't mind. It meant they were safe; no one could burgle them or take them by surprise without first climbing over and across the low walls and gardens of the ten other houses in the row.

It was nice, really.

Cosy.

Her parents had bought it when it was first built in 1893, and it remained in the family. She lived there, loved there, raised her own

---

*Fugue – act of taking flight, running away. 1: a contrapuntal musical composition in which one or two melodic themes are repeated or imitated by the successively entering voices and developed in a continuous interweaving of the voice parts in a single structure. 2: immense, dissonant. 3: a pathological disturbance of consciousness (Websters 3rd New International Dictionary) *children there and died quietly, tidily, in the back bedroom some night in 1990. She'd been there all her life and so naturally saw no reason to leave, even though she was dead.*

ii

Cardiff. Sodium city. Place of arcades and seagulls screaming in the back yard, of clear yellow sunlight and the squat red custom building, hunch-shouldered on the bay, survivor of a bombing raid. The sound of cables twanging from masts at sunset; the judder and grate of skateboards along the public art in empty squares. Place of regimented roads running alongside the railway track, where streets are named after precious stones and the metallurgical section of the periodic table: Metal Street, Topaz, Emerald. Site of historic race riots and a barely acknowledged multiculturalism, where a hymn becomes a national sporting anthem, and failure in a ball game lingers on the pavement like the smell of blood.

iii

When the neighbours asked where you were from, you were bewildered when they laughed and spoke of the strong homing instinct. 'No, *Irish,*' you repeated, thinking they had misheard. 'That's right.' A nod that indicated St Patrick's School across the street, encompassed St Paul's RC Church down the road and the Irish Catholic Working Men's Club in the other direction. 'One of the old Irish areas, this,' you were told. 'They poured in here, twenty to a room. And the fights! Scabs, they were. Strike breakers.'

Your father called you one of the wild geese, not at all disconcerted that you had found the same nesting ground generations after the first flight of the Irish into South Wales on February 2nd, 1847. That's the thing about the Irish, the immigrant. We know our history – date, chapter and verse.

Once you knew the sale had gone through and the house was really yours, you decorated. You changed the front door from cack brown to buckingham green, brightened the windows with white trim and painted the tiny front room a deep burnt orange, visible above the (compulsory if you wanted a moment of privacy) net curtain.

'Jesus,' your mother said when you showed her a photograph. 'With the green white and gold you do have it dressed up like the tricolour.'

Your scutty little house in the Grange was your first real home. You decorated it badly but enthusiastically and settled into terrace living, the meat in the sandwich, surrounded by wall-to-wall life.

'Alright, love?' the sing-song welcome and drawl of the last consonant like the drag of a high heel on the pavement. Earthy, yet slightly dangerous – an accent you fell in love with for the hint of bare raised knuckles behind the warmth.

They welcomed you, Matthew down the road giving you an education, passing through his books on Cayo and the Free Wales Army. Mai arrived with a bottle of the hard stuff and later, standing on your sofa, shot glass in hand, gave you a rendition from the Third Branch of the Mabinogi, in the original ninth-century Welsh. When CJ moved into the spare room, she brought the language with her, handmade labels of words fluttering from the door, the curtains, the walls, the table, the chair, the window . . . It was an experiment, bringing a writer to a new language with no formal lessons, but from a basic vocabulary to discover what would emerge. Fuelled by Irish whiskey, she coached you through the first hesitant sentences:

– *Mae'r tân yn llosgi.*

– *Da iawn.*

–*Mae tân cariad yn llosgi.*

And then the T-shirt legend:

Mae dynion campus yn brin.

Other gifts were as poetic. Your neighbour Keith gave you cuttings, home-grown vegetables and an example of metamorphosis. He had turned the ten-foot square concrete wasteland of his yard into an oasis: flowers, a trailing vine and peach trees trained against the new ugly red wall separating you from the estate, built on the site of the old joiners'. He grew vegetables like on the Blasket Isles, in raised beds on top of the stone, with seaweed dragged up from Barry, forest humus from beyond Lampeter and a magi-grow fertilizer, made to his secret recipe, from his own bodily secretions.

He claimed to be typical Cardiff: part Portuguese, Irish, Italian and something slightly more exotic, from a further flung soil that he hadn't yet managed to trace. Others in the immediate area professed themselves to be from Ely, Pakistan, Somali, Brazil, born and bred in that same street, or a proud 'Cardiff-coloured, me'. They celebrated March 1st, Eid, Easter, Diwali, Hanukkah, Christmas. Later, when you began to pay attention to the cultural and media representations of the city, you wondered if it could possibly be the same place.

You started to know the area, ruminated outside the Munch-illustrated 'I scream after 19 years . . .' protest house in Riverside, shopped in the North Indian supermarkets and the Caribbean vegetable shop. You lingered outside the old ballet shop on the corner of Clare Road: clothes in the window that looked as if they were modelled by dead women; satin slippers with ribbons which would never lace a Welsh leg.

You started to be known in the area, leaving your writing at the knock at the door. Laughing, lightly gossiping, you took your place outside with the other women, as children played football in the middle of the road, the smaller ones playing dolls about your feet. The moment's chat done, the watch switched over. The other women went inside leaving you mirroring them, arms folded on the doorstep, minding the kids playing on the street, even though none of them were yours.

Slowly you began to make a life there, amongst people whose talent and beauty left you dazzled and dazed.

iv

A bottle breaks, shards of glass peppering the gutter. The screel of a woman's laugh, rusty with drink, goes up from beneath your window as her companion continues his slaughtering of a song. You wake, stirring in the warmth of the bedclothes, hearing the revellers pass on up to Clare Street, then the comforting chime of the neighbour's grandmother clock. Two o'clock. Murky light

30

spills in through the window. Another clock begins its hourly song, a reprise from some pastoral ballad popular with the Victorians. Just Baby Ben to chime through the thin walls and the ritual is over for another fifty-nine minutes. On the other side, the infant cries out urgently in his sleep, prequel to a bawling, but he forgets to continue. Quiet falls with the ticking of the house's internal workings, regular as a heartbeat. You lie listening to the soft groans and creaks, the shifting embers of the fire downstairs as it carefully comes asunder. And you become aware of another who is awake like you, standing somewhere by the door, lips clamped tight over a mouth that no longer needs to breathe.

Your heart bangs loudly, then becomes easy again. You know she is there and acknowledge her presence, her right to be. As your mother often said, it is only the living can hurt us, and you relax, knowing the other means you no harm. She approves of you being here. You have turned an abandoned house into a home, brought laughter and life back into its shell.

And her being around still is no surprise. You sensed her from the first day you viewed the house, a stranger to the city, standing alone in the hallway, listening, feeling, noticing immediately the warmth, a feminine presence and that distinct smell of 'home'.

Mrs Mac.

Once they established you were not the nervous type, the neighbours told you they'd often looked over from their kitchen, straight into yours, to see Mrs Mac, several years after her body was put to the earth, at the kitchen sink. Lisa said she even waved, once. When you moved in she visually disappeared but remained there, tripping your visitors on the stairs, surprising them in the bathroom, rearranging small objects like keys, passports and wallets, which would turn up under the bed or in the coal scuttle. Although several startled friends asked who was the old lady who intruded when they were in the bath, she never revealed herself to you, which was the arrangement. You simply co-existed, sharing a love of these bricks and mortar and the occasional pre-dawn hour like this one, watching for signs of one another out of the corners of eyes. It is a lesson in cohabiting with the past, an instruction to place your ear against the thin skin of the present and listen for the city's previous lives stirring beneath.

31

Suddenly you start hearing ghosts.

You walk through Butetown and hear echoes of a violent past –
the chanting from race riots; St Paul's resounds with the smashing
of church windows where Irishmen sought shelter from the lynch
mob set on avenging a Welsh death in a drunken brawl. You pass
Howells and think of the heiress sisters – genteel militant suffragists
– sheltering women in their store when the counter-demonstration
to the Votes for Women march escalated into running battles down
St Mary's Street.

But mainly you are haunted by the Irish potato famine victims,
weak with fever, sliding over the mudflats in the Vale of Glamorgan,
wading ashore after an unimaginable passage as human ballast in
the ships going to Cardiff Docks. An illegal cargo, the destitute
Irish paying passage with their weight, desperate to escape an
environmental catastrophe, engineered by the British into genocide.
A third of the population died, a third stayed, a third emigrated to
the new worlds of Australia and the Americas through the docks of
Newport, Liverpool and Cardiff.

After the ordeal of illegal passage, many couldn't face or afford
the onward journeys; many more died. Statistics are hard to come
by, but the graves don't lie. You stumble across the cemeteries:
Brennan and O'Keefe from Skibberreen, Dennehy from Cavan,
Gilligan from Sligo, Mahoney from Galway, Courtney from Clare
and scores of others. A sudden unexpected blooming of familiar
names on slate headstones, rubbing shoulders with the ap Williams
and the Morgans and Thomases.

Those that didn't die or travel on headed for coalmines in the
Valleys. This part of your shared history was common knowledge;
from working in Pontypridd, you had been told it many times:
how the Irish arrived during a miners' strike which they quickly
sabotaged, undercutting the wages and crossing the picket lines.

The stories of those who stayed in Tiger Bay were less known.
You discover they worked mainly in the docks, shovelling King
Edwards and Jerseys on the potato wharf. You often think about
them when walking around the new Bay development. Penthouses,
the barrage, a waterside reminiscent of every other urban

regeneration project the length and breadth of the UK. You see through that to the starved immigrants escaping the potato famine, shovelling surplus potatoes from Jersey and France onto a British dock. Did they brood on the irony of life and circumstance? Were their minds picturing those who died for the want as the spade sliced through the root?

You begin to think you are obsessed, that the unearthing of this past holds no significance to the present and your understanding of the city. Then you learn that the illegal entry into Wales and breaking of strikes still leaves a long legacy. During an altercation involving a taxi and three others on Ninian Park Road in 1997, you are called a fucking mud-crawler, the Cardiff slang for Irish immigrant, circa-1848.

vi

I could tell what day it was by the synthetic smells emanating from the bakery on the Taff Embankment. Recall the numbers of six different taxi firms. Welcome in Welsh, bless in Irish and curse in English. Say 'I love you' in seven different languages but mean it in one. I could dance sets, kicking the toes from my boots one St Patrick's night in Splott, when I was lifted up to dance along the tables lining the walls in the back room of a pub. I could pay taxes. I could sit and drink weak coffee on Hayes Island at 1 p.m. on a Saturday when that was trendy, play pool at Rajah's at 1 a.m., drink at the Cameo or Chapter or wherever, loitering on the fringes, trying to comprehend someone else's notion of the fashionable. On international days, I could sing the Welsh national anthem with only three errors, those mistakes being intrinsic to the learning experience, when drunk and hilarious one Dydd Gŵyl Dewi. I could encourage literacy skills in the under-9s at the local school, where amongst the thirty-eight children in the class there were five different first languages, none of them Cymraeg or English. I could tell when there was a storm at sea, by the seagulls circling the brewery by the Taff. I could listen to stories of sailor fathers 'from the Gold Coast' anchored down with chapel-going 'real Welsh-Welsh' mothers in Butetown. I could buy samphire, cockles and

33

laverbread from the central market and a love-spoon key ring, light pull, bottle opener and teacloth. I could buy an ugly carving from a chunk of concrete from the old Cardiff Arms Park, watch *Pobol y Cwm* with confused relatives, and envy friends in Penylan who could get Channel 4. I could step around the broken glass and vomit following a match, exchanging raised eyebrows and bemused head-shakings with older denizens, agreeing that the town was indeed mad and we would all be better off safe at home. I could vote for Plaid Cymru, speak up for the referendum; write articles and autobiographical passages reflecting on Cardiff. I could be a director on Welsh boards, a Welsh university lecturer, a theatre critic for *New Welsh Review*, a serial lover of Welsh men, inspiring my friend Mai to mutter 'oh no, not *another* fucked-up Cymro.' I could learn the language, the history, the rules for rugby, take my turn minding the kids on the front step.

But what I could never do was belong.

CARDIFF QUARANTINE

Gwyneth Lewis

I was born and brought up in Cardiff, but I didn't understand the city properly until I sailed past Penarth Head and into the tea-coloured waters of Cardiff Bay.

I knew, of course, that the city was a port. My father was a Public Health Officer with Cardiff City Council and worked in the port for a large portion of his career, so the docks were part of our everyday life as a family. When I was very young he would cycle to work down to the sea all the way from Whitchurch, where we lived. In the evening, I'd climb to the top of Heol Gabriel's hill to meet him, and was rewarded with a freewheel down on the crossbar of his black bike. We heard stories about the docks at home, and sometimes wondrous vegetables, such as root ginger, found their way to our house. This was in the early seventies before Britain began to cook foreign food. We didn't know what to do with the dubious root, so it stayed on a shelf until it shrivelled. We didn't throw it away because the unpromising spice was proof that there was an exotic world with us in Cardiff, offering its dangerous taste in our own little kitchen.

My father's career started in the docks, and I have a child's memory of visiting offices at the bottom of Bute Street. I remember a large wooden chair with a red velvet cushion on it just at a child's eye level among the tall official furniture. I remember meeting Mr Eliot there, one of my father's friends and colleagues. He was very good at repairing things. It was he who mended an alarm clock that I had played with in the bath.

I was taken on visits to the docks themselves, wondrous playgrounds for a child. The equipment for shifting cargo was like a giant's toy, and there were men shouting and horribly noisy

35

machinery, the sound of metal wheels on rails, black grease everywhere and all this, even the weeds, covered in coal dust.

Of course, by then, Cardiff's days as one of the busiest ports in the world were long gone. In the seventies Cardiff was down-at-heel, and the docks were to decline even further. Despite that, I remember going down to the docks one Christmas time in the late eighties to watch a foreign ship leaving port. There was a dog on board and my father wanted to ensure that the potentially rabid creature wasn't left illegally in Cardiff. He visited the ship and then, in the rain, we watched the vessel rise in the lock and move out into the Bristol Channel. I was very interested in the small group of women under umbrellas who were waving an emotional goodbye to the crew!

In its heyday, Cardiff was a one-commodity port. It exported coal and imported iron ore and wood for pit-props from around the world. By the seventies, Cardiff had diversified and was importing a wider variety of goods. Tuna came from St Helena and oranges were a big item. The Geest boats went to Barry. For us, frozen prawns were a particular problem, and we'd often receive phone calls at home when my father had to condemn a cargo of the seafood. The British were only beginning to eat prawn cocktail and the prawn farms in the Far East hadn't yet learned not to use contaminated water to grow the delicacies. The hygiene standards of foreign farms have improved greatly since then, but my father would rather play Russian roulette than eat prawns even today.

As a child I knew nothing about life in Butetown or Tiger Bay because we lived in Whitchurch. In the late seventies young people of my age began to frequent the docks after closing time in order to visit clubs like the Casablanca and the New Moon at the top of Bute Street. I've heard a great deal about life in Tiger Bay since I married Leighton, a native of Cardiff who spent ten years in the merchant navy in the sixties. His stories about the docks were quite different from those related to me by my father!

We spoke Welsh at home, and nearly all the Welsh-speaking children of my age were the children of parents who had moved to Cardiff from other parts of Wales. Aside from the Brittens and the Daniels, who were native to Cardiff, my parents' generation had left their homes in the rest of Wales in order to work in Cardiff. This meant that the Welsh-speaking children of Cardiff had two homes: the city and the rural hinterlands of their parents. I know that the Tŷ'r Cymry (The House of the Welsh) in Gordon Rd, where the young people who were new to Cardiff went to socialise, was responsible for the marriages of a number of my contemporaries' parents. My own parents met there, and the first thing my father noticed about my mother was that she was wearing red boots (my favourite footwear too, so taste in shoes must be genetic). My mother came from Llanddewi Brefi to teach English in Caerphilly Grammar School for Girls. My father was originally from Ogmore Vale, the son of a miner and grandson of a preacher. This meant that accents from elsewhere and the life of other places were an important presence in our lives in Cardiff.

Our house, 106 Heol Gabriel, was in the middle of an estate of new Wimpey houses. We spoke Welsh at home, but the culture out on the street was totally different. At least the road was called a 'heol'. Today, cul-de-sacs on new estates are far more likely to be called Silver Birch Close or Mulberry Drive, regardless of whether they're in the Rhumney Valley or Runcorn. To begin with, I was surprised that the children in Heol Gabriel spoke a different language from me and that Elaine, Julie and Madelaine didn't understand Welsh. With the flexibility of young children I quickly learned when to use which language. But even so, there were some things that I just didn't know. As a five-year-old I remember attending a works Christmas party at the City Hall. After receiving our presents the children were required to stand in a big circle and sing *Jingle Bells*. I felt ashamed that I didn't know the words. I still don't.

The members of the Welsh community in Cardiff belonged to a small village which was scattered across the larger city. I went to a Welsh-medium nursery school and, then later, school; I attended chapel twice on a Sunday and, later on, the Urdd's Aelwyd Youth Club in Conway Road. If you so chose, you could live your life completely in Welsh in Cardiff (aside from asking for milk in the corner shop). At the end of the seventies, I remember visiting Eifionydd, the Welsh heartland, for the first time, and was astonished and upset to hear one fervent nationalist declaring that Cardiff wasn't even a part of Wales. This was pure nonsense, but it broke my heart at the time, because I wanted to be a Welsh poet.

I also had friends and interests outside the Welsh-speaking community: I was a member of the Brownies, and loved going to the Phil Williams and Sybil Marks School of Dancing. Later on, I took ballet lessons with Miss Marriott, who had a damp studio in the basement of a Charles Street building. She was a vivid character who wore striped trousers and colourful scarves on her head, and she sat like a monkey on the back of her chair, laughing at 'you gels'. Sometimes, when I was more dreamy than usual, Miss Marriott would ask, kindly enough, if I'd understood her English. The truth was that, in those moods, which she called my being 'wild and woolly', I wouldn't have responded too well to Welsh either. I was grateful to Miss Marriott for her common sense later on: when I told her that the careers person in school wanted me to be a lawyer, 'No!' she hooted. 'You're far too creative for that!'

For the Welsh speakers in the city, Cardiff was, therefore, a linguistic and a social port. Welsh-medium education was in its infancy: I attended a Welsh-language unit in Heol Llanishen Fach school before joining the pupils of Bryntaf. I don't remember any problems between the children in Heol Llanishen Fach. If you wanted to begin a new game, you put your arms round your friends' shoulders and chanted 'Join in a game of . . . "Lost in Space"', or whatever was the current favourite. It was a different story in Bryntaf, as we shared a yard with Viriamu Jones English-language primary school. There we fought, rather than playing together, 'Englies' against the 'Welshies'. I made friends once with an English-speaking girl in the yard but one day she tried to strangle me, so I was very much more suspicious afterwards.

A port is never only one place, as it is the meeting-point of at least two others. In Cardiff, the social life of rural Welsh Wales took place in a modern, cosmopolitan city which had a long history of accepting groups of very different people. When I was twelve we moved to live in Penylan. There was a synagogue on the corner of our road and we found ourselves in the middle of the Jewish community, of which I'd previously known nothing. We were members of Eglwys Heol y Crwys. This was before the chapel had become known as the 'Snobs' Chapel', and it was not much different from any other Calvinistic Methodist church in Wales. At one time we had to read and learn Biblical passages off by heart in order to win Sunday School medals. I was very relieved when this practice came to an end. I remember Sunday School trips to Aberafan and the Gower peninsula, the circle of deckchairs like a Wild Western wagon train surrounded by the Red Indians of the wind and rain.

I have a vague early memory of a Sunday School trip from Penarth to Weston-super-Mare on one of the famous Campbells' steamers that worked the Bristol Channel. Mr Lloyd Jones, the Minister, waved a white handkerchief at us as we drew slowly away from Penarth pier. I don't know why the Minister wasn't with us on the trip but I was fascinated by this theatrical gesture. It fitted in with his dramatic sermons, during which he would seem to lose his temper completely at the congregation for refusing the salvation of the Lord. Whenever I stayed up in the chapel with my father for the sermon instead of going into the basement with the children, I noticed how punctually Mr Jones modified the hell fire in his voice so that the sermon could end on time (tones of tenderness and wonder) and we could sing the final hymn happily and go home to Sunday lunch. I never trusted this melodramatic way of preaching but I'm glad that I experienced, through Mr Jones's voice, an overtone of the Big Meetings of the 1904 Revival. Capel y Crwys suffered a modern urban fate, however: it was sold to a Moslem congregation and turned into a mosque.

Among many other things, a port is a narrow place which has to be gone through in order to reach the open sea beyond. In my teens, going out with boys was the most hazardous space of all, presenting painful navigational difficulties. By now I was a pupil at Rhydfelen Bilingual Comprehensive and travelling twenty miles every day by bus from Cardiff up into the Valleys. That journey enacted the movement of goods which had created Cardiff as a port. We would travel from the coastal plain up to the narrow Valleys, alongside train tracks, past Castell Coch, where the Taff still ran black with coal dust, through Taff's Well, past the Nantgarw pit with its tip opposite, through Upper Boat and into Rhydyfelin. Long chains of open coal wagons being drawn down from the Valleys to Cardiff and the docks were still a common sight. These were the last days of the coal industry in Wales, before the traumas of the strike and the Thatcher years. By the end of that era it was people and not coal that would be the main traffic up and down the A470.

As I was a 'swot' in school, there wasn't much hope of finding a boyfriend there, but I did manage to snap up a boy who came with his friend to the dances at the Aelwyd in Conway Road. For our first date, I was invited to a *ceilidh* at the Heath Hospital Social Club. That evening I used a newfangled thing called conditioner on my hair for the first time but och, the boy brought two of his best friends with him and we ended up talking about motorbikes with them in the bar, which wasn't what I'd had in mind at all. I thought I knew what folk dancing was, as I was used to those in the Aelwyd. Little was required of the dancers other than clapping hands from time to time and galloping enthusiastically from the bottom to the top of a line. The dancers in this *ceilidh* were malevolently professional, and the dances so complex that we made complete fools of ourselves – and it mattered. 'You're home early,' my mother said when I came in at a horribly decent hour. I still bear a grudge against folk dancing.

There's no point living in a port unless you're willing to travel. I was away from home in college and in the United States, for eleven years in all, before returning to live in Cardiff at the end of the eighties. At that time I met my husband Leighton, who had been brought up in a Cardiff very different from mine: Tiger Bay, Splott and Adamsdown. He, like me, loved the combination of the small and large in Cardiff. It is a small city and works in many ways like a village. The first thing my mother would always ask me after I'd come back from town on a Saturday would be 'Who did you see?' In London, I can never get used to the fact that I don't bump into people I know: though this has happened, it's not the norm. And yet Cardiff has the confidence of the well travelled. Its people know at first hand about Suez, Japan, Nycotcha and Canada. I love this combination of the intimate and the expansive, the dear and the terrifying, the local and the global in one place. As I drove to the chapel with my father to my wedding, it was very important to me that we should be passing places that I had known all my life before launching out on the wider and strange waters of marriage.

I'm not quite sure how the sailing started. Leighton and I had thought that we might buy a small dinghy to sail at the weekends. As a Christmas present I bought him a Competent Crew course with a sailing school in Cardiff Bay. By this time the developers were about to start the construction of the Cardiff Bay Barrage, to which I was strongly opposed. Leighton took his lesson in a January gale and was hooked. I went on the same course later in the year but it was a dismal failure. The moment we motored out of the Ely River and turned past Penarth Head to put up the sails, I started to feel seasick. We sailed down to Swansea and back in two days but my sickness didn't improve. 'Look, Gwyneth, there's a lovely view of Southerndown behind you!' somebody would say. 'Not interested,' I'd say grimly. 'I'm not moving my head for anything.'

A decade later, we're living on a boat and sailing abroad to visit some of the ports with which Cardiff traded in the nineteenth century. The seasickness isn't much better, but now I take pills for it. Our attempt to understand more about the nature of ports has so far taken us from Cardiff to Milford Haven, through Falmouth, Brest, Lorient and across the Bay of Biscay to La Coruña in Galicia and down the Atlantic coast of Spain and Portugal as far as Lisbon. I've learned a great deal about the history of the sea and about what is required in order to enable you to travel safely and comfortably in turbulent waters. I'm only beginning to understand the relationship between sea and land, between ports and the distant places which make them thrive, between the idea of 'over here' and 'over there', what is home and what is truly foreign to us. After all, no culture has traded with foreign countries without being irrevocably changed by those distant places. Great Britain imported much more than goods from her Empire, she imported a whole new population and way of looking at the world. And if ports are places where attempts are made at regulating travel and trade between nations, they are also places where the most serious international problems manifest themselves: disease, racial violence and crime. A port may provide shelter from bad weather but it can also be a dangerous place for the sailor. It's a place that meets a sailor's needs but which also exploits them. A port is a paradoxical place. It's a home and a symbol of everything that's alien. It's safe and also dangerous. It's a way of sending things out into the big world and the means by which the world steps in over your own threshold.

Today, Cardiff docks have almost completely disappeared. Cardiff Bay is the new entity in which yuppie flats look out expensively over the freshwater lake which glints in front of the proposed building for the new National Assembly for Wales. I was in favour of locating the Assembly in the Bay, in the hope that the new institution would profit from its location in a port and its valuable combination of native values and international hospitality. After all, a port is a local place which nevertheless understands the international language of the sea. Perhaps sailing into Cardiff should be a compulsory part of the new Assembly Members' induction (I know of some very good seasickness tablets). And looking at the horizon for a long time never did a person anything but good.

STAYING POWER

Leonora Brito

Incident #1

After my mother had her first heart attack, she and my youngest sister were seated quietly inside the ambulance, while the paramedic monitored her heartbeat.

'So, where you from then?' asked the paramedic, quite matey.

'Over there,' said my sister, nodding towards the corner house.

'No,' said the paramedic, smiling. 'I mean where are you *from*?'

'That house over there!' said my sister, pointing emphatically.

'Oh forget it,' said the paramedic in a huff.

My mother looked at my sister and found herself laughing, in spite of the heart monitor. She said, 'We knew what he was getting at.'

Incident #2

Ten or so years ago, I won first prize in a Wales-wide short story competition. The Welsh TV actress there to present the prize beamed at me and my family as she shook my hand, and enquired sweetly: 'Do you speak English?'

Neither of these two incidents is particularly unusual or even hostile. And I present them here as examples of everyday encounters and exchanges between people in Cardiff who happen to be black and people who happen to be white. Actually, the TV comedy actress was a North Walian down on a visit, but she found it easy to make the assumption that *we* were the outsiders, not her. I didn't enlighten her, and the occasion passed off quite pleasantly, with the actress declaring we were all *'lovely!'* as we were leaving (perhaps because my mother had asked for her autograph, which she then lost before we got home).

But for what it's worth, I was born in Cardiff and my mother was born in Cardiff, as was her mother, my grandmother. My father, Antonio Brito, came from São Vicente in the Cape Verde islands; so did my mother's father, my grandfather, José Silva. For as long as I can remember, I have always known where I was 'from'. Necessarily so, because as a black Cardiffian, the two questions I'm most frequently asked are: (a) Where are you from? and (b) I meant, where are you from, *originally?*

And yet, Cardiff's history as a maritime port and city has snaked its way through my own family's history for over a hundred years. And here's a potted biography of my grandmother to prove it:

I was born Doris Mary-Ann Harris at Number 22 Francis Street in the Docks area of Cardiff in 1908. My mother came from a little village called Muchelney in Somerset and her name was Ellen Tremlett before she married. My father's name was Bill Harris, and he was born on Snap-apple Night in 1877, and he died on Guy Fawkes night, when I was seven. He was a boiler-maker, working on the ships. All his family came from the Docks area of Cardiff. His brothers were paper-hangers, decorators and painters – that's how our front door in Francis Street had a brass knocker and a special teak finish.

My mother used to work for an Italian ship chandler: she used to clean and cook for them, after my father died. She made good faggots and peas too, and sold them. I was an only child, and she liked to dress me up. I always had decent clothes to go out in. My best frock when I was small was of dark-blue velvet, with a light-blue satin sash at the back.

My best friend's name was Edna Ellis, and she lived across the road. Most kids used to play in the street; our favourite games were gobs, marbles and swinging from the lamp-post on a rope. Sometimes we played in the park in Loudoun Square. Older people used to play tennis there, and bowls. But we liked to go and look at the fountain. I remember there was a plant that grew around it called snow-on-the-mountain.

Every summer my mother took me on holiday to Somerset, where two of her sisters still lived. We used to take the pleasure steamer from the Pier Head to Weston-super-Mare and sail across; it was cheaper than going by train.

School? I didn't like school, Board School. I was a terror in school. When I left at fourteen, I found work in Dame Wales's Flour Mills in Tredegar Street, packing and sealing. I remember my mother let me keep the whole of my first week's wages. She was always good to me. And on the weekends, when I was of age, she'd let me go dancing. She didn't mind, as long as I was home by ten o'clock. All my friends were Spanish then, and I used to go to Spanish houses.

There would be these little 'dos', for the Spanish and Portuguese mostly. And we'd drink cups of coffee and dance Spanish valses and Argentine tangos. I loved the tango most of all. Though sometimes we'd do the military two-step. It all depended on the gramophone records that were brought along. I met my husband, José Silva, at one of those little dances. He was a good-looking man, and I was a smart young woman. When we got married in 1929, my mother decorated the front room with streamers of ribbons, all different colours.

I spent my married life in Number 21, Francis Street, and although my first husband died when he was thirty-five, I lived there until the street was demolished in 1964. The day they knocked it down, a lot of us came and stood on the corner of Canal Parade and watched. And I remember I cried because of all the memories that came into my mind.

Call me perverse as a writer, but what I like most about my grandmother's story is its overwhelming sense of ordinariness. And in the context of where she lived, her story was unexceptional, varying in its specifics, but similar to that of countless others. Here are two further recollections, both of a cross-cultural nature, so to speak:

In the days following her marriage, my grandmother fed my grandfather on what amounted to a succession of Chinese takeaways: 'I used to get him rice, prawns and bamboo shoots, from Sam-On-Yen's, because I thought he'd only eat foreign food. After about a week, he said he wouldn't mind trying potatoes, meat and veg.'

The only political statement I ever remember hearing her make was during the Falklands War, when she fulminated: 'Why don't they give those people their islands back – the Malvinas!'

My grandmother died at the age of eighty-seven, having lived her life in the same small area of Cardiff. Once, on a visit to America, she was asked her opinion of California, which was by then the adopted home of her second daughter, my Auntie Val. My grandmother told her surprised listeners that California wasn't a patch on Cardiff. 'It'll never come up to it,' she said, 'never!'

High praise, but I feel sure the Cardiff my grandmother was extolling was her Cardiff – variously known as the 'Docks' or 'Butetown' or 'Tiger Bay'. Which was not, of course, the dangerously exotic, nefarious and essentially fictional place so often conjured up by (mainly) male writers for popular consumption. No, hers was an altogether more mundane spot that resembled if anything a friendly, spiteful, gossipy, yet neighbourly, village.

Back in the 1950s, the 'village' was an overcrowded, often dilapidated one. And by 1959, it was the relentless, hugger-mugger quality of day-to-day living that my mother was looking to escape from. She'd spent the first five years of her married life living in rooms. Two rooms, front and back, in an early Victorian terraced house around the corner from her mother, in Christina Street. My brother, my sister and myself were all born in that house, which we shared with our Malayan landlord, Kaddi, and another young family, headed by a seafarer named Limbo who practised becoming a jazz trombonist in between trips.

In the summer of 1959, we were offered a house in Llanrumney, a newly-built council estate to the east of the city. My father was away at sea, and it was my mother who said yes to the offer and set about organizing our momentous move. I'd just turned five on the bright summery day we left the Docks. I don't remember any tears, only a mood of excitement and adventure as my brother and I were hoisted onto the back of Billy Douglas's open lorry and deposited in the family armchairs, one apiece. Then, like the Clampitts heading for Beverley Hills, we were off.

Halfway up Rumney Hill, my mother's youngest sister Marjie pointed to a strip of silver that kept appearing between the house-tops and the sky. She told us it was the sea, something we'd never seen before – the Channel Sea! Then, three miles further on, at the bottom of a wooded hill, we reached our house.

It was one of a line of four, built of pinkish red brick, with mortar that looked like icing sugar. We had a front garden with a pretty milk-white gate, that lowed like a metallic cow when we swung on it. And in the middle of each garden the council had planted a special council-house tree, that only grew halfway. Ours was to blossom every spring, overburdened with cluster upon cluster of small pointy petals, that were as vividly pink as the coconut in raspberry ruffles.

Amidst this child's-eye view of things, what stays bright in my memory is the general air of well-being reflected in the adults around me. Our neighbours, like ourselves, came from the older parts of Cardiff: Adamsdown, Canton, Newtown, Grangetown. They'd been living in rooms like we had; or with in-laws; or in houses that had been 'condemned.' Everyone spoke constantly about the fresh air 'out here'; and seemed to feel their move was a good one.

If there were any shreds of meat on the bone of Harold MacMillan's contention that 'people had never had it so good', then they were to be found here, in Llanrumney. Put there in large part by Cardiff City Council. Inside each house there was a two-ringed gas cooker, a boiler for boiling up clothes, and a useful little gadget that looked like a long, dry cinder of coal with a hose on the end of it. This was called a gas-poker, and once lit its blue-tongued flames could keep a fire going until it caught.

I learned from my mother, seeing through her eyes as she engaged in the naming of things in our brave new world. She was especially keen-eyed when it came to nuances of colour: the freshly plastered walls of the tiny living room she pronounced to be buttermilk yellow, while the duller yellow of the fluted fireplace wasn't dull at all, it was ochre, to 'set it off.' In contrast, the front-room fireplace had cool, misty grey-and-blue flecked tiling, with grey-blue walls 'to match'.

I think it was the newness and excitement of setting up home that kept my mother going in those first few years. For most of that time my father was away on long trips at sea. And if she was ever lonely or nervous (as she must have been) – a young woman not

47

yet thirty, set down on the edge of the countryside with three young children in her care – she rarely showed it. Instead she bolstered her confidence by drawing on memories of her Somerset grandmother.

Grandmother Ellen had carried her country ways into the city, making, among a host of other things, her own elderberry wine, and raising ducks, then chickens, in the back yard of Francis Street. These she efficiently despatched by slipping a carving knife down their gullets and 'wraggling' it from left to right. My mother confined herself to growing tomatoes in our back garden, and planting a row of hollyhocks and marigolds (her grandmother's favourite flowers) out the front.

I remember her picking the tomatoes while they were still stubbornly green, and wrapping them in tissue paper. Placed in a box in a dark space under the stairs, the tomatoes emerged a week or so later magically ripened to red. They were tart to the taste, but would do, she said, for salads.

Most of the families around us, internal migrants three or more generations removed from the soil, seemed eager to try their hand at growing things. And while the fields beyond the estate remained empty apart from a few cows, the patchwork of back gardens especially were quickly awash with criss-crossed bamboo poles, little sheds and greenhouses, and stretches of protective green netting.

One of our neighbours built a pigeons' coop; another, a sunken pond. Summer nights you'd hear the croaking of frogs; and virtually every night, it seemed, the strange throaty cooing of at least a dozen roosting pigeons.

In 1963, my father came ashore permanently. Until that time I knew him more through the collection of things he'd sent 'from sea' than by his presence. The word 'father' only conjured up a broad-brimmed hat, a belted, tea-brown mac and a big scuffed leather suitcase.

Yet the collection of things that he sent home – I'm thinking in particular of an ornately-decorated Japanese tea service (each cup when held up to the light showed the hitherto hidden face of a Japanese lady); a beautiful black lacquered musical box; a junk ship; a chalk-white army of holy statues, lighters and ashtrays; and curiously ugly sea shells that lit up at night – helped us to define who we were. Having them on display in the glass-fronted cabinet or along the window sill put clear blue water between ourselves and other families. In our own eyes at least, they made us different in the sense of 'special'.

Mostly this was down to my mother, a lifelong romantic when it came to the 'sea' or 'abroad'. For her, these were magical, incantatory terms whose very vagueness conveyed a sense of the illimitable possibilities of life. Reverencing the 'sea' and 'abroad' was her way of giving expression to the other side of who she was – a woman whose long dead father had been a sailor from somewhere called Cape Verde, and whose husband carried the same history.

But my father wasn't much of a romantic when it came to the sea. A man of few words and many a critical silence (brought on by harsh experience), he never indulged in tall, colourful tales and seemed constitutionally incapable of waxing lyrical whenever my mother plied him with questions about the place where he was from, or the many places in the world where his ship had docked. He gave bare-bone answers, but she kept on asking, gleaning bits of information over the years.

He'd been working aboard ships since the age of fourteen, usually below deck in the engine-room as a donkey-man greaser. During the war he'd sailed the dangerous Atlantic runs, bringing Argentine beef to meat-starved Britons. Not that he spoke much about it, except to recall that the first time he saw snow, he'd thought it was something the Germans had dropped. Another time he spoke sardonically of seeing with his own eyes dead bodies piled up in a harbour somewhere; and reading next day in the newspapers about a failed German U-boat attack. 'That's propaganda,' he explained. 'Government propaganda.'

But this sort of loquacity was rare. The skin on both his legs had pink and brown scarring like tortoiseshell where they'd been scalded by oil. 'Engine-room accident.' End of story. A further accident in 1963 left him unable to find another ship in what was by then a declining industry. So, in his fifties, he had turn to and find work ashore.

Luckily there were jobs aplenty on dry land in 1963, and my father quickly found work as a labourer in a metal die-casting factory. It was always something of a mystery to my mother how easily he turned his back on the sea. Yet he settled down without regret, and even took up gardening in his spare time. I remember him coming home one Saturday afternoon with two polythene-wrapped rose bushes under his arm and a cricket bat for us kids (which, alas for the Tebbit test, we used as a baseball bat). In due course, our front garden became enclosed by a thorny but tidy hedge; wild pink roses entwined the porch railings; and my father managed to grow a variety of vegetables in the back garden, until he decided the soil needed a rest.

It seems ironic in view of all this that his dark presence appeared to set the seal on our 'difference' as a family, in that we became more readily viewed by others as indelibly alien. But perhaps I was just growing older. 'Don't touch that hedge,' I remember hearing one boy say to another as they gathered itchy pips. 'That's a black man's hedge!' As kids going about our daily business, we were subjected to constant casual name-calling from other kids, what is now termed racial abuse. We learned to hit back, but by the time I reached junior school I began to harbour a secret dream of one day returning to live down the Docks, where life would be miraculously happy and uncomplicated.

When we finally moved out of Llanrumney, I doubt whether race was an overriding factor. True, that after about ten years, my parents began to talk nostalgically about the place they'd left behind, their nostalgia tinged with a practical sense of loss. Shops stayed open till all hours down the Bay, and they sold all kinds of food, like salt fish, chickpeas and chorizos. And yes, people were friendly down there. But mainly it was inconvenient living so far out.

In the end, we were only able to move nearer town (like most of our neighbours) rather than back to the Docks. The place we moved to was if anything even less welcoming in a racial sense; but we were able to live with that. Like most black Cardiffians, we'd discovered that acceptance as such is usually conditional, and like the weather, always subject to change.

CITY OF TALL STORIES

Gillian Clarke

War. Radios. The sea. A fox. Stone animals on a castle wall. I can't say what came first, but in an undated long-ago a boy dived from a bridge into black water. It smelt mossy, like a well. My father held me on the parapet while I sent pennies spinning into sunlight before they fell, drowned in tree shadows and the sunless waters of the canal. Brown boys, and boys as white as the marble boys in the Museum, jumped into the void hugging their bony knees, and came up blowing water from their noses, sometimes with gold in their fists. Some of my pennies must be down there still, in the feeder canal under Kingsway, dragged by a slap of water or the splash of a rat, deep under, where they will never be found.

It was a game for a Saturday morning outing, just me and Daddy. Part of the fun was fear of the drop, the black water, the tunnel, my skin tingling, my heart jumping like a frog. I would put myself to the test, stepping to the edge of any vertiginous darkness before legging it, or hanging there, safe, in my father's arms. The mind's equivalent was 'Who made God?' Tucked up in bed after a story, I would ask myself the most frightening question in the world, or allow myself to think about forever and ever until I had to shout for someone to come. According to Ga I was always asking about God, as her letters to my father and his sisters testify. I was never given a satisfactory answer.

Risky places, the deep, the dark, the edge, where looking down makes your head spin, and looking up turns the earth. This was the enchanted place, where the canal eeled under Kingsway towards the Castle ramparts draped with the tails of peacocks, and its wall with the seventeen-stone beasts that, according to my father, came to life to prowl the city by night, and where the ghost of Ifor Bach still raised his flag on the tower when Wales were playing England. I wore my new coat with a brown velvet collar, mittens on a string, a hanky in one pocket, my pennies in the other. My father's coat was whiskery tweed and felt like the fur of the black bear in the tobacconist's shop near the Prince of Wales Theatre where, before dirty films and Bingo, they showed *Snow White*, or *The Wizard of Oz*, or *Lassie Come Home*.

An outing in the city of tall stories. First, my father's office in the BBC in Park Place, with its tall commissionaires, studios, wires, microphones and mysteries. Then the Museum. Later, perhaps, to his favourite cafe in Caroline Street for egg and chips, or down Bute Street to the pub whose name I forget. Everyone knew him in these places. Sometimes we walked streets with wonderful names: Womanby Street, or Golate, where, in the olden days, sailors used to go late to embark on their ships for places I could touch on the globe at home; Westgate Street, where, in the future, from a corner of the BBC box at the Arms Park, Cliff Morgan and Onllwyn Brace would become heroes.

In the Museum the Blue Lady's dress is so blue it is a lake of bluebells in Porthkerry woods. So blue that she's the sea off Pembrokeshire. Because of her, blue is my favourite colour. Once I'm seven, I'm allowed to wander the lofty halls, the staircases, the galleries opening out of galleries in this wonderful place all on my own, while my father checks something in his office over the road. In the Museum the woman in her Welsh costume cooks *cawl* and Welsh cakes and *bara brith* forever over the red coals of the stove in her lovely old-fashioned farm kitchen. In the Museum the fox steps from its den beside a glass stream, one paw raised, its glass eye gleaming.

It is as real as the fox cub, quivering, hot, with a thrilling smell, that my father carried home in his coat through the bombed streets, all the way home from the office in Park Place. He walked in the dark on broken glass up Cathays Terrace, across the junction of Whitchurch Road where people were running and crying, past the Carnegie Library, the cemetery, the park, the lake, up the hill and all the way to 1 Cyncoed Avenue where, once upon a time, we all lived together: me, my mother, my father, his mother (my Mamgu,

52

'Ga'), his sister Doris who was never to be called 'Auntie', her husband Uncle Howard, and my father's eldest sister Ceridwen, known as Ceri, who once tried to run away with a married man, but was stopped by my father at Cardiff railway station. 'Worst thing I ever did,' he said time and again throughout Ceri's troubled life. Auntie Phyllis, the middle sister, Great Western Railway clerk from Carmarthen, self-taught teacher of speech and drama, was a frequent visitor, bringing books and reciting Shakespeare and the Psalms, and telling me not to talk so fast and to watch my enunciation.

I still feel the quivering heat of the cub, but what I see of my father's walk through the shelled city came later from a letter to his mother, my Ga, safe at Fforest, the family farm in Pembrokeshire. The farm was kept going, just, by Jim the bailiff and, for a while, two Italian prisoners of war, Raphael and Mario, who had motor-bikes and let me ride pillion. They were good men. Nazis were bad men. Once, on the A48 near Bridgend, my father pointed to a prisoner being walked on the verge. 'That's Rudolf Hess,' he said. 'A Nazi officer.'

The family came and went between Cyncoed and Fforest like a wandering tribe, Howard between his offices in Cardigan and Windsor Place, my father travelling the country as OB (Outside Broadcast) Engineer for BBC Wales. After the night of the broken glass, he took me to Fforest to be safe with Ga by the sea, where the war was just a bad story on the wireless, a winter storm, Bendigeidfran raging at the waves. It was at Fforest in the lawless west that Doris skimmed cream from the tops of the churns in the dairy, and sent me for eggs from hen house and hedge for her delicious cheese sauces; where they laughed, conspiratorial and safe in the farm, to hear that the local policeman called my father 'the whitest man in the black market' for supplying his friends at home with contraband eggs and ham – imported to Cardiff once, they said, in a hearse, and where my uncle was fined for 'watering the milk'.

I couldn't date or explain it, but once, earlier, 1940 or so, my father carried me up the gangplank onto a ship in Cardiff docks. My glamorous mother followed. ('So pretty she took our breath away,' the chemist in Cyncoed told me years later.) She wore high heels. It was night. We climbed down steep steps into the ship's belly. A beautiful man met us. He was the Belgian Captain, my father's friend from the days when he was a ship's wireless officer for the Marconi company before he met my mother and joined the BBC. The Captain gave us a mango. The juice ran down my chin. The sea lapped at the porthole. The cabin rocked. When I woke up I was in bed at home and thought I'd been dreaming, except that the next day I watched my mother plant the big mango stone in a pot. A beautiful stone, like the keel of a little ship, draped with the golden fibres of the fruit. It never grew.

Our house in Cyncoed was 'the first house on the meadow'. An elderly neighbour told me so when, years later, at twenty-two, newly married, I returned there to live in the upstairs flat. No other house has established itself in such detail in my mind. I lived there at crucial periods of my life, times when heightened awareness of the indoorscape lays down rich memories: earliest childhood; the first years of marriage; the birth and upbringing of three children. Other places left the outdoors more strongly imprinted on my mind – Fforest especially, where rocks, sea and cliffs, woods and waterfall, shippon and hayloft are clear and detailed, while the farmhouse interior remains vague. 1 Cyncoed Avenue was familiar in the complete meaning of that word, a house I can never leave behind. I recorded this in a sequence of poems called 'Cofiant' ('Biography'):

> Houses we've lived in
> inhabit us
> and history's restless
> in the rooms of the mind.

It works both ways. I can enter that house right now, because it is a part of me:

> How can you leave a house?
> Do they know, who live there,
> how I tread the loose tile in the hall,
> feel for the light the wrong side of the door,
> add my prints to their prints to my old prints
> on the finger-plate?

How, at this very second,
I am crossing the room?

I still recall learning to walk on the oak parquet hall-floor, the
pleasing rattle of the few loosened blocks under my feet. We lived
downstairs with Ga. Doris and Howard and sometimes Ceri lived
upstairs. When Doris and Ceri quarrelled, Ceri would rant and wail
and depart in a huff to live in a caravan in somebody's field. As the
house resettled into itself, the consensus was 'Good riddance'. She
was always welcomed home after a month or so.

I lived mostly in the garden in a black pram with a white silk
fringe on the hood. Trees trembled over my pram. I know now they
were poplars. Their roots reached under the clay, shrinking and
surging with the weather, cracking the walls of the family house
they had built for £700. Uncle Howard was an architect. He built
the Art Deco Plaza cinema, and the Bowling Club with the
undulating roof that collapsed under a heavy fall of snow in the
eighties, and his own house in Sherborne Avenue whose interior,
even as a child, I loved. I suppose it must have cut a dash at that
time, a modern house in a suburb of traditional dwellings, stylish,
all blond wood and pastels like the colours in Art Deco cinemas,
ivory, apple green and old rose sharpened with dashes of black,
and a white baby grand piano that nobody played.

It was Doris and Howard who introduced me to the theatre, the
footlights, the opening chords of the orchestra, the rise of the great
curtain. Every Boxing Day they took a box at the New Theatre for
a family trip to the pantomime. My sister and I wore party frocks
for the occasion.

My mother, who aspired to the privileges conferred by
education, yearning for them with a hopeless air of personal
disappointment, handed me a mixed bag of gifts and deprivations.
She taught me to read before I went to school, but she banned
Welsh. Her own experience as one of ten children of a Welsh-
speaking family demonstrated that a tenant farmer's Welsh-
speaking children were poor, while a landlord's English-speaking
family were rich. 'I want you to get on in the world,' she said.
According to her, the South Wales in-laws laughed at her North
Wales Welsh. Maybe, but life had made her over-sensitive, and

vulnerable to South Walian humour. She sang me nursery rhymes, taught me the names of wild flowers, let me stay up late to listen to *Saturday Night Theatre* on the radio, and *Jane Eyre* serialised on Friday nights, and planned the doubtful blessings of elocution lessons and boarding school, if I didn't shape up. My father set the stories of the *Mabinogi* in locations wherever we happened to be – in Fforest, in Cyncoed, in Kingsway, in Roath Park. He took me to the Arms Park, and the opera. First, *The Magic Flute*, in one of the theatres and cinemas that used to flank Queen Street. Auntie Phyllis took me to *Peter Pan* in the New Theatre, and got me a week off school every year to visit Stratford. My first Shakespeare play was *King Lear*. I was ten, and wept for the old man who broke friends with his daughter.

One day the family story would fall into place, the 'real' become distinguished from the myth. I eavesdropped on grown-up talk in Welsh and English, voices over my head which seethed with rumour, gossip, quarrels, scandal, malice, stories, the Bible, Grimm, Hans Andersen, the *Kathleen Fiddler Omnibus*. My father's stories on the slow road between Cardiff and Pembrokeshire as the danger of bombs came and went. Words. Delicious words. Names. Coed ar hyd y Glyn. Splott. Golate. Brains Dark. Coedpoeth up north where Nain and Taid lived, and Gobowen, and Wrexham Lager Beer. Once at Fforest, balancing on the slippery wall that dammed the flow of slurry between the shippon and the sloping yard, I was muttering favourite words, collected into a couplet, stamping its syllables as I went:

> Ga puts mentholatum on her sciatica
> And Ceri soaks the clothes in Parazone.

Parazone. I fell. Ga shouted. Someone carried me squirming like a piglet to the pool under the waterfall where clean little shadows of freckled brown trout darted away as I was plunged, shouting, in icy water, then carried me home, rinsed of muck, to be bathed by Ga in the scullery sink and dried by the fire to wait for Daddy to come and hear the sorry tale.

We moved from Cyncoed to Barry. Ga came too. 'Flatholm', Lakeside, Barry, our own house overlooking Cold Knap Lake. It was a white house with a flat roof and bay windows that followed the curve of its prow like a ship, and a flagpole where my father ran up the Y Ddraig Goch to flutter in the wind off the Bristol Channel as if we were, indeed, aboard ship. Doris said the house was the height of style. Both my parents had left school at fourteen, Llanelli Grammar School and Grove Park Grammar School, Wrexham, respectively, the only surviving son and youngest child of a rural railway man, and the daughter of a tenant farmer: where did they get such ideas, and aspirations to what they could not afford? I knew they couldn't afford it. Doris said so. I worried.

Soon after that I had a sister, five school-years younger than me, enough to give us separate childhoods. Eat your egg, there's a war on. Bombs fell on the docks. A piece of shrapnel made a hole in our dining-room window. A German shell hit a ship with a cargo of oranges at Barry Docks, and broken crates littered the shore of the Little Harbour. Trained early to forage in food-rationing days, we children staggered home with our jumpers, skirts and knickers filled with fruit, the first real oranges we'd ever seen. One night my father woke me and took me to the window of my bedroom over the porch to see the lights of hundreds of planes flying overhead. And, in Llandough Hospital, Ga died, my last sight of her in her blue dressing-gown blowing kisses from a high window.

They sold 'Flatholm' – because of money, said Doris – and after months in lodgings in 'Felden', The Parade, we moved to Penarth, first to Cwrt-y-vil Road, and soon to 'Oaklands' in Plymouth Road. The plan was that I would go away to school, and my mother would turn the house into a guesthouse. I loved the big square rooms, the secret corners, the oak floors and turn-of-the-century stained glass, the large walled garden, ruined greenhouses, old coach house and stables, and the glimpse of sea from my bedroom window at the top of the house. Years later I learned that Oaklands had once been the home of the painter Ray Howard-Jones. My father spent his every spare minute keeping it from falling apart.

We could see the sea from Cyncoed; from a few hundred yards away at Fforest Farm; from 'Flatholm'; and from my attic bedroom in Plymouth Road. From my Cyncoed bed I heard the steelworks thump in the dark and trains going East, and a colony of tawny owls in the woods and fields that would become the Llanedeyrn estate, where a woman was murdered while out blackberrying. It was never solved. She and her basket of fruit still haunt those acres that look east over the Rhymney. From my cot in 'Flatholm' I heard planes, and RAF men rolling home after Saturday dances at Bindles. In Penarth the call of the Breaksea lightship on a foggy night most moved me, one long moan before its voice broke. Then again.

And always the sea. Voices. Rows downstairs. And radios. Wireless sets, they used to call them. Behind glass in the lit cave of each of our many radios was a needle, and with that needle you could navigate the world just by turning the knob. Later, on the bridge of a ship, holding the wheel tight, trying to keep the needle on a steady course, I remembered those first voyages by radio, through the languages, the crackling wastes of ocean between Cardiff, Athlone, Hilversum, Moscow, and home to *Children's Hour.*

Nothing could put me off the sea, or water, even that early baptism of body and soul under the waterfall. I had to be hauled out of swimming pools by attendants, and called from the sea by Ga or my parents. Cold Knap Baths, Penarth Baths, the sea at Fforest. Even the lost boy didn't stop me, though his ghost haunts every narrow place where the sea sucks or where water flows underground. The cover came off an exit pipe at Cold Knap Lido, and a boy was drawn into the pipe, where he drowned. And turned to marble. A boy called into the mountain by the Pied Piper. A girl from my class at Romilly Road Junior School, Barry, a traveller's child from the caravans, was taken and murdered. Two other children were found half-buried in leaves in a wood. *The Mirror* or *The Graphic* or *The News of the World* headlined the story 'Babes in the Wood'. My mother hid the paper but I saw it. Story became life, life became story. It happened far away, but for me it was Porthkerry Woods, with bluebells and the sound of the sea, a train crossing the viaduct and my feet running down dry woodland paths and out over pebbles in broad sunlight where my mother was unpacking the picnic.

Stories layered with stories, all laid down in the mind to become part of being.

It's often said, and it's true: children were free then. At the age of eight or nine we'd leave home after breakfast and not be expected home till dusk. We (my friends and I) walked along the beach from Barry to Porthkerry. We made fires. We built dens in the wild wood between the park and school. We got deliberately marooned on Sully Island – a peninsula when the tide is out, but an island at high tide. At ten or eleven years old, I and a friend would cycle from Penarth to Cardiff, under the subway from Penarth Dock to Ferry Road, then up through Grangetown, the Castle grounds and on to Rhiwbina woods, or over the mountain to Caerphilly. We caught trains to unplanned destinations. Best of all, I would wait at the end of the pier in Penarth, alone or with a companion, for a Campbell's steamer bound for Weston or Ilfracombe. At dawn, with a queue of other voyagers, leaving my bike chained to the pier, I would wait for the boat to hove into view. *Glenusk*, *Glengower*, *Ravenswood* or *The Bristol Queen*, or, best of all, *The Cardiff Queen*.

When, at eleven, I went to boarding school in Porthcawl – another of my parents' unaffordable aspirations – for the next seven years Cardiff became The Weekend and The Holidays. Weekends we'd go shopping, my mother, my sister and I, in the big city stores. My mother was always entranced by the glow and glamour of department stores, Howells and David Morgans and Evan Roberts. While she bought fish at the still famous stall in the Market, I'd slip upstairs to see puppies in the pet stall, and browse in second-hand bookshops, finding once a copy of *The Maid of Sker*. I wanted to read it because of Lorna Doone, and because it had familiar places in it – Newton, Sker House, and Tusker rock.

Then we'd go with our treasures to have tea in the Angel or the Royal, fingering the papery packages, sniffing our wrists for free perfume trials, looking at a *Vogue* dress pattern, a bolt of floral cotton, items from Haberdashery or Lingerie – Oh the words! – reading *Woman's Own* and *School Friend* over tea and cakes. I'd have a new school blouse from Roberts, maybe a library book, some romance I hid from my mother – *The Sheikh*, something by Ethel M. Dell. There was no such thing as teenage fiction, and no transitional literature between childhood and adulthood.

Libraries had always been full of objects of desire. To a

bookworm, there is nothing so bleak as the last page of a book an hour before bedtime, and nothing more thrilling than the Saturday morning find in the library, a new novel by a favourite writer, or something illicit, and hours of secret reading ahead. It was almost a vice. From early childhood I'd read all night, unable to stop turning pages. In school I read under the blankets by torchlight. Home for the holidays, sent to make the guests' beds in the roomy old house in Plymouth Road, I'd be caught reading the books on the bedside tables.

One weekend, home from school, at Doris and Howard's in Sherborne Avenue, I staged my first political demonstration. The first among us to have a television, they invited us all to watch the Coronation. I sat on the window seat, 'nose in a book', while my mother complained that I was 'missing history'. I declared myself a republican. When I did sneak a look, I saw a grainy grey picture, the white face of the new Queen lost in the rain.

In my O-level year, my father fell seriously ill. After an operation, he took six months' recuperation leave from the BBC, and went to Patagonia as a supernumerary on a banana boat. While he was away, and I was mostly at school, something changed in my mother. Her disappointment at his lack of promotion into management in the BBC had embittered her. He came home for Christmas looking tanned and well, but it was a bleak season. I saw that he was estranged in his own home. He had brought home taped recordings he had made among the Welsh-speaking people of Patagonia, talking, and singing in their eisteddfod. The BBC refused to use the tapes because my father was an engineer, not a programme-maker. I sensed deepening disillusion. Forty years later, in the Museum bookshop, I looked up my father's name in the index of John Davies's *Broadcasting and the BBC in Wales*. Writing about the BBC's prejudice against its own Welsh-speaking staff, John Davies quotes their treatment of my father:

> J. P. K. Williams, appointed assistant maintenance engineer at Cardiff in 1928, was denied promotion because the superintendent engineer 'did not consider that the Welsh temperament (was) as suited to supervisory duties as the English temperament'.

I was standing in the lofty foyer of the Museum, which I'd loved all my life. My father had been dead thirty-seven years. I felt a bomb go off in my mind. My mother's bitterness was justified. These bigots had blighted our lives.

We five 6th formers were the first university entrants from St Clare's Convent. My father was ill again. Money had run out. My sister was away at school. Instead of going away from home to university, I went to Cardiff on a county scholarship, and travelled daily from Penarth.

I was in love with the very idea of university, and relished my new life. Cardiff was suddenly glamorous. I was grown up, an undergraduate. I loved the Civic Centre, the ornate white buildings, the rose-red road of Edward VIIth Avenue where I walked to college every day under huge elms that touched overhead. Later, they were all killed, every one, by Dutch elm disease. I saw them felled. It was like watching a great cathedral fall.

On my first day as an undergraduate, I walked from the station up Westgate Street, Castle Street, Kingsway, under the cloudy elms of Edward VIIth Avenue, through the Gorsedd Gardens, up the crescent of the drive, under the porch and into the cool spacious hall of the university building, excited and terrified that now I'd arrived I would have to speak to someone.

Just being in the library with an essay to write, books spread on the table, the sentences shaping themselves, made me feel I was on my way. By day, when I wasn't at lectures, or lounging with new friends in the women's common room, in the Student's Union or the Kardomah, I liked to stay on in the city as long as possible. If I went home there'd be housework to do, my father to worry about. I'd be back to my old life. So I'd work on in the lovely university library in Old College, whose generous space barbarians would later destroy with an ugly mezzanine floor. In the evening, after a cup and a scone at the Hayes Island Snack Bar, where tea was poured into ranked cups in a continuous hit-and-miss stream, I worked upstairs in the old Central Library, where a tramp snored over a book and pigeons cooed on the window ledges – sounds I still associate with books, with reading, with falling in love with the idea of study, and with English Literature. In the same way, sitting annual exams became associated with the banners, bands and choirs of the Miners' Gala passing down Queen Street on a hot June day.

Was I really working? I put the hours in, certainly, and got a kick out of writing a good essay, all the while wired to the presence of male undergraduates – the ratio was four men to one girl in those days. The library stairs were good for swirling a circular skirt with a flicker of broderie anglaise beneath, the table in the alcove perfect for imagining, under the guise of studiousness, that the handsome student at the next table might be looking your way.

Learning for learning's sake would, we were told, give us the world. This seems amazing now. I don't think many students feel the romance of university that we did. We knew we were privileged and were grateful for it. I was no scholar, but I loved English, language excited me, and reading gave me other worlds. My fellow undergraduates were mainly from the Valleys, miners' children, all of us backed by whole tribes of relatives, all excited to be pioneers, to be young, to be the generation given the big chance. We were the granddaughters of the Suffragettes, the children of Nye Bevan and the Welfare State. We were political. We voted. We demonstrated. I listened, dazzled, to Michael Foot speak passionately and brilliantly in Crwys Road Chapel. It was obligatory to wear academic gowns to lectures and in town, so we were a conspicuous group. Cardiff belonged to us. The places where we consorted, flirted, romanced, sorted the world out, planned the anti-Suez march, anti-war or anti-nuclear demonstrations – the Students' Union, the Kardomah, the Hayes Island Snack bar, the pubs, the Old Arcade, the 'Woody' – put a new, grown-up Cardiff under my skin and into my bloodstream.

In May, in my second year, my father died in a nursing home on Penylan Hill. His last words to me were, 'Hwyl fawr, bach.' All the bigwigs of the BBC attended his funeral.

I graduated, got a job with the BBC in London, and after eighteen months of being a stranger with a funny accent, I came home to Wales for good to marry my boyfriend from university days, and to live in 1 Cyncoed Avenue again. Our children were born there. We remained married for ten years, and then, not surprisingly, found we were not who we'd been at eighteen and twenty-one respectively, and we grew in different directions, while remaining friends, remaining family.

We sold the house in Cyncoed in the 1990s. It was a painful moment, and a moment of freedom. We sold a house and an attic of skeletons. I cut ties, and shed a lot of luggage. My daughter and sons, all born to that house, two in my parents' old bedroom, had grown up and left home for art college and university. My life had shifted west to my ancestors' country, to a new life. I visited the house where I was born less and less. I'd found it was possible to live somewhere else, without ever leaving behind the city that was in my bones. I kept what I wanted, left the rest in the skip in the road.

It's my daughter's city now, and her children's. The new Cafe Quarter is a step from the Market and the Hayes Island Snack Bar. There is a new hum of confidence, and somewhere called Cardiff Bay that we called 'down the Docks'. But listen to the voices, the gossip, the nosiness, the unstoppable cheek and humour, the interrogation of strangers. Take a taxi. 'Where d'you live? West Wales? There's lovely. Got a caravan in Tresaith. Small world.' We are driving past the castle towards Kingsway. I ask, 'Which is your favourite animal, on the wall?' 'I likes the bear.' 'Me too!'

MINORITY REPORT

Grahame Davies

I can still recall the exact moment when I realised my daughter had become a real city kid. At six years old, she was telling me how she was planning – for some date in an unimaginably distant future – her wedding. It was fairly predictable stuff – a white dress, a church, a big party.

'And what would you have to eat?' I asked, humouring her.

'Well . . .' She mused for a few moments, probably considering, so I thought, the relative merits of pizza and chicken nuggets.

'Well, couscous, of course.'

Of course.

I think I was probably over thirty before I knew what couscous was. And, to be honest, I'm still fairly hazy about what it's made of. I think it's some kind of wheat. Or it may be rice. It's North African anyway. I think.

This episode made it clear to me just how much my world had changed. When I was growing up in Coedpoeth, a former mining village just west of Wrexham in north-east Wales, the closest we got to exotic cuisine was Vesta's boxed cook-it-yourself Chinese meals, with crispy noodles and a tiny sachet of soy sauce. Another more common treat was to be found at Borras Park chip shop in Wrexham, where the ingenious owners served a delicacy so unusual that it was sufficient to bring people like us down from the surrounding hills from miles around to sample it – chips with onion gravy.

Not that we were badly off. My father was a building contractor and my mother a journalist, and we lived in a big modern detached house. It was just that, in those days, in the 1970s, there seemed to be far fewer choices, whether of food, television programmes, or lifestyles. In a village like that – similar in many ways to the mining communities of the south Wales Valleys which I later came to know very well – the culture shared by most people, whatever their income bracket, was closer to what we would now regard as working-class.

Cardiff never figured in our world. Liverpool was our big city. It was there that our relatives went to work; it was on Merseyside that my father spent a good chunk of his childhood; it was Merseyside's local TV programmes that we watched every night. Only when Shotton steelworks closed in 1980 was north Wales mentioned on TV, and our pride at having been featured for once on *Look North* almost took the edge off the pain of the eight thousand job losses. It was to Liverpool that we would go on shopping trips, or to watch football games, or, in my teenage years, to see heavy metal bands at the Empire Theatre. And in due course, when I came to apply for a job as a journalist, it was to Merseyside that I looked, applying first of all to Liverpool's *Daily Post* and to Radio Merseyside – unsuccessfully in both cases. I would no more have thought of applying for a job in Cardiff than for one in Caracas. It just wasn't on our horizon at all.

And yet, a few months ago, while I was at my daughter's school fair in the grounds of a church in Pontcanna, I found myself chatting to a friend who was also brought up in my home village. As we exchanged enquiries as to the health of our various relatives back home, it struck me that there were two more of my school contemporaries from Wrexham in that same small gathering. Four of us, brought up a hundred and fifty miles away, all had children at the same Cardiff primary school. And if I thought about it, I could name four more classmates from my own small comprehensive school who were now down here in Cardiff. Clearly, something major had changed since our teenage years.

I first visited Cardiff shortly after Mrs Thatcher came to power, when I travelled down by train to attend my father's Open University degree ceremony at Cardiff City Hall. The politics of the period were impressed on my memory by the fact that I shared the train with a large group of protesters heading for a 'People's March for Jobs' rally which was being held in response to the first wave of job losses inflicted by the Tories' scorched-earth policies.

Later that day, as we had tea in a first-floor cafe in town, we saw the marchers go along Castle Street, and I looked down on the red-haired figure of the young Neil Kinnock, familiar to me from his TV appearances during the recent 1979 devolution campaign. Rebelling against his own Labour Party's plans for a Welsh Assembly, he had led a hugely effective spoiling campaign, in which the estrangement between north and south Wales, between Welsh speakers and English speakers, had been ruthlessly exploited. North Walians were warned against domination from the heavily populated Socialist valleys and from a distant, alien, Cardiff; South Walians were warned that Welsh speakers would descend from the north to rule the country. Quite how a 20% minority was going to dominate the other 80% of the population through a democratic institution was never made clear; but fear was stronger than logic. Those divisions contributed to the 'No' campaign's crushing victory in the referendum. Four out of five of the electorate voted against a Welsh Assembly.

If I am to conform to the nationalist stereotype, I should say how I felt despair, anger and betrayal, how I vowed to continue the struggle by other means. That kind of thing. But personal stories, like those of nations, are complicated, and the truth is that I was quite complacent. The whole thing felt like a rather satisfying rebuke to the earnest ethos of the Welsh-medium secondary school which I attended at the time.

My conversion to the cause of Welsh self-determination would come a few years later, when I was eighteen. I had transferred from my Welsh-medium school to an English-medium sixth-form college where I was the only Welsh-speaking boy. Suddenly I was the odd one out, and I realised how tenuous my hold was upon the language which, although both my parents and all my older relatives could speak it, had not been the main language either of our home or of our community. So when, in 1982, the jingoism of the Falklands War yomped across our collective consciousness in a blur of camouflage colours draped with red white and blue, I realised with a shock who ran the country, and how they ran it, and why. And I realised it wasn't my people who were in control, not the Welsh, and certainly not the Welsh speakers, who, I now realised, were a small, marginalised, fragile and exposed minority.

We counted for nothing. If we were to survive, we were going to have to struggle. That realisation, and the determination stemming from it, has never left me.

So, did I spend the eighties painting roadsigns and refusing to pay television licences then? I'm afraid that, as a campaigner, I was the equivalent of football's 'sub not used'. I did join Cymdeithas yr Iaith Gymraeg (the Welsh Language Society) for a year, but my career as an activist never really came to anything. Invited by letter to a 'cell' meeting in a pub, I turned up ready to be initiated into the clandestine world of civil disobedience. But no one else showed up, and I came out of the pub as law-abiding as I'd gone in. Then, in response to another invitation, I set off to Colwyn Bay for a protest at the constituency offices of Welsh Office minister Wyn Roberts. I misjudged the distance, though, and by the time I got there it was all over. Not exactly battle honours, then. I never so much as saw a paintbrush raised in anger. Undeterred, I planned to go to Aberystwyth University, where I was going to throw myself into the language movement. But my poor A-level results meant no Welsh university would take me, and I ended up in an arts college in Cambridge, removed from the struggles of the language civil rights movement and the miners' strike which were raging back home as the challenge between communities and capitalism became starker and more desperate. Despite my best efforts, I seemed compelled into conformity. I did collect money for the miners, though. In Cambridge. In between lectures.

It was in the immediate aftermath of the miners' strike, during the freezing January of 1986, that I came to live in south Wales. While in college I had pursued my ambitions to be a journalist, was accepted by the Thomson regional newspaper group as a trainee, and, after a course in Newcastle-upon-Tyne, was posted to work on one of their south Wales titles, *The Merthyr Express*. I didn't even know where Merthyr was: I had to look it up on a map. But I was to spend the next ten years in the town, and, as the Tories worked out their belated revenge on the unions who had broken their government in the early seventies, I looked on as the valley's four pits and the Dowlais steelworks were closed and demolished, and thousands of people were forced into a twilight world of benefit books and bitterness.

I found the Valleys communities very similar to those of industrial north-east Wales, where I had grown up with the rumble of Brymbo steelworks as a constant backdrop. I felt an immediate empathy with the situation in the Valleys, and this was expressed in the poetry which I produced at that time: angry stuff that condemned the way these industrial communities had been exploited and forgotten.

My early poems, published only in magazines, had dealt primarily with the tensions of being brought up in a border area. But it was the experience of the Valleys which produced the work that was later collected in my first volume of poetry, *Adennill Tir*. The title, which means 'Reclaiming Land' or 'Land Reclamation', was an ironic reference to the Welsh Development Agency's hoardings which appeared on former pit sites and slag heaps all through the Valleys at that time, proclaiming bilingually: 'We are reclaiming this land for new use.' I liked the strangely subversive implications of this proclamation, and used it in my poems as a metaphor for the political and cultural resurgence which I longed for, but never expected to see. Although by duty an optimist, I'm cursed with an instinctive pessimism.

I finally moved to Cardiff in 1996. During the decade I had spent in Merthyr, I had married a Valleys girl, Sally, who had been a fellow reporter on *The Merthyr Express*; we had had our first child, Haf Morlais, born in 1994. The 'Morlais' was chosen because it had local connotations, but Haf never got the chance to demonstrate this loyalty of nomenclature to any great degree, because, before she was three, we had moved away. I had already been working in Cardiff for some years by then, first for *Wales on Sunday* and then, from 1991, for the BBC. Gradually we found we had more friends in Cardiff and little reason to keep commuting from twenty-five miles away. We joined the drift southwards.

Simply choosing to live in a working-class Valleys town like Merthyr had seemed like an act of solidarity in itself. An illusory activism by virtue of location. That status quo was to be challenged very starkly when we moved to Cardiff. Now in my thirties, I was to encounter a culture shock greater than any I had previously experienced. Perhaps the shock would have been less startling if we had chosen to live in a different part of Cardiff. We chose Pontcanna, but not because of its reputation as the home of Cardiff's beautiful people, a kind of Greenwich Village with harps – we didn't know Cardiff well enough to be aware of that. We chose it because it was handy for the shops and close to town. Nevertheless, helped by a coincidental series of professional promotions, we were now part of the Welsh-speaking media circle in this particular corner of CF1.

All the same, I should stress that, although there is a comparatively high concentration of Welsh speakers in the Pontcanna area, the actual proportion of them relative to the rest of the community is still quite small. I doubt if we're more than ten per cent of the population of this area with which we're so strongly identified. Nor are we talking about fabulous wealth. If you want the real money in Cardiff, take a drive through Lisvane or Cyncoed, or out into the Vale of Glamorgan where you can cruise past the mansions of the seriously rich, precious few of whom are Welsh speakers. But the curiosity of Pontcanna is that it does represent an unique concentration of people who are comfortably off and who speak the Welsh language.

This is a very good thing for anyone who values the continuance of the Welsh language: if Welsh is to survive, it must inhabit urban territories and adapt to modern ways of life. The fact that it is quite clearly and successfully doing so in Cardiff is something which I wholeheartedly support. Also, for Welsh to be associated with aspiration and economic advantage is a crucial factor which will assure its future. But it was still a shock. These Welsh speakers weren't scratching a living from the soil as they should have been. Some of them drove Saabs and Alfa Romeos, wore leather trousers, or Gucci sunglasses costing more than their grandmother's weekly pension. Some of them spent more on a hairstyle than the average weekly income of a hill farmer. Some of them handed their children over to childminders and private nurseries while they themselves chased two incomes. Some even had cleaners. Such a lifestyle is, of course, the norm for people in that income bracket throughout Britain, whatever language they speak. These people were nothing exceptional. What bothered me was not so much the trappings of comparative affluence, but, in some cases – and only a few – a seemingly wilful avoidance of the radicalism and communitarianism which had characterised the much poorer areas from which the majority of them had, at some point or another, moved to Cardiff.

I felt guilty. Not only had I never gone to jail for the cause of Wales, here I was enjoying a lifestyle I had never previously envisaged. I felt worried too. Welsh speakers might not belong, like black or Asian people, to a visible minority, but, as speakers of a language other than English, they belong to what I might call an *audible* minority, and, like all minorities, they can attract hostility.

In recent years, criticism of Welsh speakers *per se* has thankfully become politically incorrect. But the fact is that diversity will always be a problem for some people. One of the ways in which people who would balk at the idea of being thought prejudiced against a minority nonetheless find it possible to criticise Welsh speakers is by identifying them with privilege, thereby making them a seemingly legitimate target. I was afraid that the brashness and cockiness of a few Welsh speakers might alienate the majority community among whom we live, and would erode the goodwill that is so vital to our project of maintaining our culture within the hegemony of a larger Anglophone society.

It was this kind of consideration which fuelled my second volume of poetry, *Cadwyni Rhyddid*, (*Chains of Freedom*) which came out in 2001. This time, the dominant tone was not anger but mainly satire, aimed at exposing the tensions and hypocrisies of the lifestyle I myself was experiencing, and attempting to stress the need to reconnect with the roots of the radicalism which has traditionally characterised Welsh-speaking society. My target was that minority of affluent Welsh speakers who seemed in danger of losing touch with their roots.

The book's title was an ironic reference to the aftermath of the devolution referendum of 1997. From the moment it was announced that devolution would be made subject to a referendum, I felt like a man approaching the gallows. It would be 1979 all over again. Even with the fairest wind, a weak and disunited 'No' campaign, a slick and well-funded 'Yes' campaign, and a thumping pro-devolution vote in Scotland first, there was no way that it was going to be anything other than a 60-40 'No' vote. I would have put money on it. This time, it would really sound the death knell for Welsh hopes of nationhood, and put an end to efforts to sustain the language. With doomsday scenarios playing themselves over and over in my head, I brooded on the prospect that my daughter's first language could, by the time she was middle-aged, have declined to a point where it would be evidently unsustainable in the long term. My fears produced the following poem, 'Traddodi' ('Tradition'):

Beth ydw i'n wneud iti, mechan i,	*What am I doing, and you so young*
yn rhoi'r Gymraeg ar dy wefus di?	*Putting this language on your tongue?*
Ai rhoi cynilion oes i'th ran	*Will the lifetime's savings I'm passing on*
a fydd yn ddiwerth yn y man?	*In a few short years be used and gone?*
Ai teg dy rwymo di fel slaf	*Is it fair to give you, and you so clean,*
â chod genetaidd llinach glaf,	*a dying nation's poisoned gene,*
a iaith dy hwiangerddi clyd	*and give you, in a lullaby,*
yn ddedfryd oes o boenau'r byd?	*a world, for you to watch it die?*
Fy ngeneth, maddau'r ffŵl o dad	*Daughter, forgive this fool who knew*
a roddodd arnat faich ei wlad,	*he passed his nation's grief to you,*
a chofia, pan fo'r rhwymau'n dynn	*and when the chains are tight, then know*
mai'r reddf a'th greodd fynnodd hyn.	*the love that made you willed it so.*

My wife Sally, who mercifully did not share my pessimism, was active in the 'Cardiff Says Yes' campaign, which consisted of a group of around twenty people who represented the capital's hard core of devolution activists – an alliance of Labour, Plaid Cymru and Liberal Democrat members, in addition to some previously non-aligned individuals. But it was an uphill struggle. Attitudes were slow to change, and awareness of the issues was sometimes minimal. Campaigning in Splott market, Sally said to one passer-by; 'I hope we can count on your vote on Thursday.' 'Oh, I don't think I can vote, love,' he said, looking troubled. 'I'm from Ponty, see.'

The extraordinary sequence of events on the night of the count, when Wales voted 'Yes' by a wafer-thin majority, marked an irrevocable change in the Welsh psyche. And soon the change was to be made tangible in the physical environment of the capital city of a newly devolved nation. New investment was sucked in as the devolved administration set up shop and as lobby groups, consultancies and organisations of all kinds relocated to Cardiff in order to be as close as possible to the Assembly, which would now be administering billions of pounds of public money.

All of which was fine. But I was still troubled. As I said earlier, the middle-class tensions I satirised in *Cadwyni Rhyddid* were the same as those of people on comparative incomes in Islington or Notting Hill. But for Welsh speakers, the issues carry extra weight: we expect a lot from fellow members of our community. In our attempt to preserve an indigenous culture within an all-powerful and all-pervasive Anglo-American world, we're playing for high stakes, and we can't afford to let material comfort sap our determination to survive. I was afraid that we could win the war but lose the peace.

As I write this piece, the results of the most recent census (2001) are still being digested. The proportion of Welsh speakers in Cardiff has nearly doubled over the decade, to more than 30,000 people – ten per cent of the population; the proportion in Wales has risen by two per cent to over twenty per cent of the population, the first such rise for a century. But in the traditionally Welsh-speaking areas of the west, a slow decline continues as young people move out to seek jobs, opportunities and homes they can afford, and weekenders, retirees and downsizers take their place. But the overall picture is more hopeful than I could have imagined a decade or two ago. The game's still on, and the focus is gradually shifting to the capital city, where an unmistakeable Welsh-language urban culture is evolving. It's currently reinforced by migrants from the north and west of Wales, but it's also approaching sustainability within its own demographic resources: to take one indicator alone, the city now has thirteen Welsh-medium primary schools and two Welsh-medium secondaries.

My daughters, Haf and Alaw, are in one of those primary schools, along with a couple of hundred other kids from both Welsh- and English-speaking homes and from a wide range of social and cultural backgrounds: white, black, Asian, Muslim, Christian, agnostic. But all fluent in Welsh. The children think this variety – urban, multicultural, bilingual – is normal. And it is. It is only people like myself, brought up within the old geographical and social boundaries, who might still find it remarkable.

Which brings me back to the couscous. The world of these children seems a long way away from the rumble of the steelworks of both East Moors and Brymbo; it's also a long way from a monoculture of any kind. And mercifully, it's a long way from the political, social and material disenfranchisement which we have previously taken for granted. I am finally feeling cautiously optimistic about the world in which these children will grow up. I just hope they never forget how good chips taste, especially with onion gravy.

PESACH, 1943

Stella Schiller Levey

I was five when the last bomb to fall on Cardiff destroyed our home. It was the 18th of May 1943, and the clocks stopped at 3.40 a.m. We lived at Rosendale, 37 York Street, Canton, in a row of over forty terraced redbrick houses with stamp-sized front gardens. Ours was bordered by a golden privet hedge. The bomb also destroyed Numbers 39 (the Turners'), 41 (the Ginns') and 43 (the Wornhams'). Luckily, Number 41 was empty, as the Ginns had just moved out.

My sister Marilyn was eleven and my parents were both thirty-nine. My father, Sydney, who had been in the army stationed in Grimsby and billeted in Cleethorpes, was at home with us. When the bomb fell, he had just undergone an operation without anaesthetic and had been discharged from the army on health grounds.

When the sirens screamed their first warning, my mother Freda ran upstairs.

'Get up, quickly,' she said. There was no time to put on our navy blue all-in-one siren suits which had been made to keep us warm in the air-raid shelter. There was no time to get to the damp, mouldy Anderson shelter at the bottom of the garden. When Dad had dug the shelter, we had 'helped' by carrying away buckets of earth. He had dug deep until he was able to put a corrugated steel roof over his pit, then we'd helped him put all the earth back on top, and covered it with turf until the whole thing looked like a giant molehill. Mam had protested that it would flood at the first rain and we would all die of pneumonia.

'*Geschwind!* Hurry!' Mam urged us into the Morrison shelter in the downstairs front room. A wire cage with a steel top, it was pushed against one wall, with two sides exposed and the fourth open for us to get into it.

The sirens screamed again. Dad was chatting to our elderly neighbour, Mr Turner, a soft-brogued Irishman, who loved to natter on the doorstep. Because we were Jewish, the street nicknamed us 'the Cohens and the Kellys'.

'Come in *at once*,' said Mam. She didn't need to raise her voice. Not a person to panic, Dad reluctantly strolled into the lounge and crouched down to crawl into the shelter.

'Let's pull the settee across the opening,' Mum suggested, and she helped Dad to tug it up to the shelter to act as a fourth wall. Then she hurled herself on top of my small body, pressing me tightly to her and calming my frightened whimpering. 'Hush now, *mein Kind*. Don't make a noise or the Germans will hear you.'

A loud silence filled the air.

'*Shema Yisroel Adoshem Elohenu, Adoshem Echad,*' Mam murmured. It was the first Hebrew prayer I had ever learned in praise of the Almighty: we uttered it in times of stress or thankfulness. 'Hear O Israel the Lord our God, the Lord is One.'

Then our world exploded. Windows, doors, ceilings, roof, slates, chimneys – all yielded to the blast. The settee was hurled against the far fireplace wall linking our house to that of the Hanmers at Number 35, and it was dashed into matchwood pieces, as if it were fated to be a sacrifice in place of our four rigid, terrified bodies.

We huddled together for an eternity, breathless, praying, waiting. The exhausted air, thick with dust, hung immovable around us. The 'all clear' wailed into the shattered night like an open-throated wolf baying at the full moon. Alarm bells jangled. Help arrived. A torch's beam flashed over us.

'Anyone in there?' The gruff voice of the ARP (Air Raid Precautions) warden sounded strangely beautiful to us at that moment.

'Yes, four of us,' Dad replied.

'Any injuries?'

'All well, *Gott sei dank*,' said my mother.

'Good-oh. Be with you now.'

My parents cocooned me in an eiderdown, handed me carefully through the tattered blackout curtains and jagged glass in the window-frame and I was passed along a chain of eager helpers through a bomb-torn space in the bitter-smelling golden privet hedge that had been my mother's pride and joy. Another parcel followed – my sister.

'Tom.' I heard my father call out to Mr Turner. York Street was a row of terraced houses and the Turners' front door was only inches away from ours. Dad called again, but in vain. The Turners, unable to reach their garden shelter in time, had crouched under the stairs and the house had tumbled down on top of them. They were dead.

Only the previous Friday, Mrs Turner had knocked on our front door bearing a flat parcel wrapped in brown paper and tied with string. 'Mrs Schiller,' she said in her soft Irish accent. 'I've brought you a white tablecloth. It's from my trousseau and I've never used it, no, not once, in over forty years. I want you to have it.'

'Oh, no,' my mother started to protest, but Mrs Turner waved her down.

'You're not to argue, my dear. You are a God-fearing person and I respect your piety. I want you to use this cloth every Friday night for your Sabbath Eve table. No arguments,' she held up her hand. 'I know you will put it to good use in the service of our Lord.'

My mother was, for once, speechless.

'What's more,' Mrs Turner continued, 'I want you to do me a favour. I have a feeling that Tom and I won't survive this war.'

'How can you say that?' Mam replied. 'You must have faith in the Almighty.'

'I have, my dear, but my premonition is strong. I want you to promise that, if anything happens to Tom and me, you will look for this handbag,' and she gestured towards the shabby brown leather bag dangling from her wrist. 'In it are the deeds to our house. They are for Grace. Olive is married. She's taken care of, but Grace must have them in the event.'

'I promise,' my mother said, her eyes brimming. 'Though I pray it won't be necessary.'

Mrs Turner embraced her. 'If it's the Lord's will . . .'

Now, frantic, my mother sought out the ambulance driver. 'There's someone there – you must dig. Their daughter's in the house – or perhaps she's in the garden shelter. You must keep calling out to her.'

'No, lady, nobody can be alive in that wreckage.'

'Well, we were,' she snapped. 'You must look for her. Grace! Grace! Can you hear me? It's Freda Schiller.' Mam darted fearlessly among the debris, calling her name over and over. Arms reached out to stop her but she dodged them, persisting. Suddenly she halted, listening intently, head to one side. Then she called out triumphantly, 'All right, Grace. It's all right. I can hear you. You'll be safe in a moment.'

Mam ran back to the men standing around the space that had been our home and the Turners'. 'Start digging. She's alive. Grace is alive, I tell you.'

They dug their spades in and moved heaven and earth in minutes. There before them lay the mangled body of our neighbours' young daughter.

'She must be dead by now,' someone muttered.

'No.' Mam stood there, indomitable. The men looked at her as if she were mad.

'No, she's alive. She's been spared. God is good.'

At those words Grace's eyes fluttered open and a feeble 'God bless you' escaped her dust-caked lips. The men lifted her carefully into the ambulance. 'Find the handbag!' Mam commanded, and Dad started digging.

Meanwhile, police officers opened car doors and bundled Marilyn and me inside.

'Where are you taking them?' Dad asked.

'To the rescue centre in Cowbridge Road,' one replied.

'I don't want that,' my mother said robustly. 'My brother's down the road, in Lansdowne Road. Number 196. I want them taken there, please, while I go in the ambulance with Grace.'

'Okay, missus.'

The black police car glided down York Street carrying me and my sister. A gas main had burst in the middle of Lansdowne Road, and a mammoth bonfire halted our path. Lurid orange and red tongues of flame shot up out of the gas main into the dark night, and human figures stood around it in a circle, silhouetted like cut-out paper dolls. The police car ran out of petrol and the policemen had to carry us down to Uncle Joey's. As Auntie Gertie put us to sleep in her bed, Uncle Joey ran down to York Street to stand guard with Dad against the looters who had already started their dirty work.

From the wreckage of our home some furniture could be saved: the dining-room table, four chairs and two carver chairs and a sideboard, and the bedroom furniture, all made of solid oak.

When the front room fell in during the bomb blast, none of the glassware on top of the shelter was broken, neither was the china cabinet nor its contents. Like us, they had been spared.

Being a very young child I suffered no trauma; I just had all the images in my head. All the same, to this day I can't bear listening to any kind of siren. Marilyn, however, suffered greatly from the sound of aeroplanes flying overhead: even before our own home was hit, she used to run out into the garden or into the street, terrified – so much so that my parents had decided to send her, for a short time, to a Jewish hostel, in Cefn Coed, Merthyr. She was supposed to stay until the end of the war with children dispatched to the countryside away from the London bombings. She had been home on holiday when the bomb fell and never went back to the hostel.

So you see, I survived the Blitz – just. My name is Stella J. Schiller. The J stands for Judith, which my Mam wanted to call me, but she thought it might be shortened to 'Ju'.

'Ju, Jew,' she said. 'It'll encourage anti-Semitic remarks.' That was a chance she didn't want to take, as the news coming out of Germany and Poland was increasingly grim. Instead, she called me Stella (meaning 'star'), and Judith became my second name.

I was born on the fourteenth of August, 1937, under the sign of Leo. My birth took place in the Eton Nursing Home, Eton Place, not too far from our home in York Street, which was flanked by Cowbridge Road at one end and Lansdowne at the other. The Swansea-Cardiff-Paddington railway line ran behind Lansdowne Road, and it was this line that the Germans were aiming for when the bomb landed on our home. York Street was in Canton, a district that took over from Riverside on the west side of the river Taff on its way up to Victoria Park.

My first memory of life at 37 York Street was, in fact, my first memory of war. It was The Day War Broke Out, on Sunday, 3rd September 1939. The weather was fine, so Mam and Dad had taken Marilyn and me over to Weston-super-Mare for the day by boat, leaving from Pier Head, Cardiff, and calling at Penarth Pier on the way. We didn't know then that such a sunny summer's day would turn out to be one of the darkest days of the century. We certainly didn't think we would hear and see enemy planes flying overhead and bombs being dropped nearby. It all became too close for comfort.

Every night was a blackout night. Light from houses drew enemy planes like dreadful moths so we all had to have curtains made from thick black material to keep any light from filtering through the windows. Even then lines of yellow light became beacons in the pitch black and an air-raid warden would knock at the door to tell you off. You lay in the deep darkness in your bedroom even if you were scared of the dark. You just had to be brave: it was part of the war effort. No street lamps were turned on at night, and you walked with a torch pointing downwards to show when you stepped down from a pavement or back on to it. Car headlights were covered with gummed brown paper with only a slit of light permitted. People with window blinds painted them black and we all had strips of brown gummed paper criss-crossed over the windows to stop them shattering.

Mam always took her prayer book with her into the shelter. I would see her lips moving in prayer as she opened it to a well-worn page and I wondered if God could hear her.

One terrible day a big brown envelope with no stamp on it was delivered to the House. Dad was ordered to attend a medical. Suddenly he was in the army and sent up north to Cleethorpes. While he was away, Marilyn and I couldn't go to synagogue on Saturdays, our Sabbath, and we were not permitted to travel on the holy day. Nor could we attend Hebrew classes on a Sunday morning or after school, as Mum had to cope alone with us and, of course, we had no transport. Dad's car, a black Austin with a KG registration, was laid up on blocks in a neighbouring garage. This meant that we didn't mix with any other Jewish children other than our two male cousins. Mam felt it was her bounden religious duty to instruct us. We learned all the necessary blessings, and we went through the entire Sabbath service with her, singing along with her beautiful soprano voice and bowing reverentially where necessary.

Mam paid a Jewish teacher, Mrs Baram, to teach us our Hebrew letters. She came on Tuesdays and Thursdays after school. Often we were instructed by candlelight if there was a chance of a bombing raid. When the sirens roared, she would become hysterical and scream, 'I want to go home to my husband.'

'Calm down, Mrs Baram,' Mam would say. They were so formal in those days.

Mrs Baram would end up sometimes in our shelter until the bombing was over, weeping copiously and wringing her hands until the 'all clear' sounded. But we learned how to read and write Hebrew.

In April 1943, the family gathered in my grandparents' home at Number 11, Fitzhamon Embankment, Riverside, to celebrate *Pesach*, our festival of Passover, when we give thanks for our freedom from slavery in Egypt. My grandparents' house stood in a terraced row. The tall dresser on the right-hand side in the back living room displayed shelf upon shelf of china, and a black Rexine sofa stood under the window on the opposite side. A pantry opened off one end of the room and at the other end a new fireplace had replaced a bomb-damaged black stove. In the centre of the room stood a laden *Seder* table. The two *Seder* nights are on the first two nights of the eight-day festival, when Jewish people all over the world, however weak their belief in the practice of Judaism, try to get together with their families and follow the rituals of the service.

A starched cloth with knife-edge creases gleamed white; the reflections of flickering candles danced in the tray beneath their silver-shod feet, and glasses of ruby-red wine awaited the first sip. We sat around this table with an air of expectancy: me (aged five), my older sister, Marilyn, on a home visit from Cefn Coed Hostel; our parents Freda and Sydney; Auntie Rae Goldberg; Uncle Joey Danovitch and Auntie Gertie with our cousins Ralph and Bernard; our 'adopted' American soldier, Walter Lenner, who was stationed in army barracks in Wood Street where the Millennium Stadium now stands, and the German refugee, Benny Eschwege, who lodged in the attic room with his bicycle for company.

The door opened dramatically from the narrow hallway and my majestic grandmother, Rose Anna Danovitch, whom we children called 'Bubie', the Jewish pet name for Grandma, led my ailing grandfather, Gavriel, Zeidie, slowly to his seat of honour at the head of the table. He was dying – although I never knew it. Little girls were sheltered from such words as 'death' and 'cancer'. Zeidie's weary bones, wrapped in paper flesh, sank weakly into an inflated rubber ring placed on the seat of his carver chair for comfort.

Zeidie used to wheel Bernard and me in the pram, with Marilyn and Ralph holding on the sides of the handlebar as they walked, to get us away from under our mothers' feet on a Friday morning when they were busy preparing for Shabbat. And on the Shabbat afternoons, he set up an arrangement with the owner of the Trico Ice-cream Parlour on the corner of Cowbridge Road and Victoria Park Road East to supply all of us children with two-penny Lyons Maid Ice-cream rounds from which you unpeeled the paper before placing it in a cone. He would go round to pay for them on the Monday: we weren't allowed to handle money on a Shabbat, as this would have made it a commercial transaction on the day of rest.

Zeidie had come to Cardiff in 1904, the year of my mother's birth, to see how the land lay. More and more Jewish people were fleeing Poland because of the pogroms, and some of the family had already come to London. I don't know why he chose Cardiff. Maybe he already had friends there who had told him there was work to be had. So he left his wife (my Bubie), Reisel Ghana, which is Yiddish for Rose Anna, at her mother's home in Warsaw, together with baby Freda.

Soon, however, Zeidie wrote to Bubie to arrange her passage on a boat to Cardiff. Armed with a nine-month-old baby and accompanied by her sister-in-law, Chaya, plus several of her children, they boarded the boat and endured a terrible journey. Chaya ran out of food for her children and Bubie felt she had to deprive herself in order to help feed them. No wonder Zeidie was shocked at the sight of baby Freda, who must have looked half-starved. He fed her pieces of chocolate to try and fatten her up.

Zeidie had lost both of his parents back home in Staszow and had even paid for poor Chaya's wedding. What money he had left went towards renting a shop in Cardiff town centre, where he sold gas mantles for lighting. Bubie used to serve in the shop while Zeidie took himself off to the Valleys by bus, laden down with suitcases of mantles. They later moved to Bridge Street, and a further move eventually took them to a house in 11 Fitzhamon Embankment, Riverside, where they stayed.

Only weeks after we celebrated *Pesach* in 1943, we were homeless because of The Bomb. We survived, and Zeidie demanded that all four of us – Mam, Dad, Marilyn and me – lined up in front of him so that he could see that Mam was telling the truth – we were all alive. But the shock hastened his death three weeks later, on 12th June. It was the first day of *Shavuot*.

Young Marble Giants in the Casablanca

John Williams

I hitched back to Cardiff in the summer of 1979 and found myself in a city I didn't recognise.

I was just eighteen years old and I was fresh from a three-day Magic Bus ride from Greece. For the past year, since I'd left home, I'd been living in London, bouncing around the squatlands. Before that, the Cardiff I knew was the Cardiff of childhood: a city mapped out for me by my parents.

My father's family is old Cardiff, John Williams of Cardiff, steel stockholders from Victorian days. We lived by Roath Park, or up in Cyncoed and Lisvane, old St Mellons and Penarth. My mother's family came from Gwaelod-y-Garth and Somerset. They lived in Cathedral Road, in the house where I was born.

Growing up, I knew a genteel Cardiff: tea with my grandmother in Howells or David Morgans, films at the Park Hall or the Capitol, boating on Roath Lake, shopping in Marments and Maskreys and Marks & Sparks.

Later on, in my early teens, I got to know the city centre a little better, and started to venture into the dirty bookshops of Bridge Street to buy American Marvel Comics, scarcely less disapproved of than the other merchandise. I bought records from the immortal Spillers, Buffalo, Sound Advice and City Radio with its listening booths, and jeans from Gentle Folk. I went to my first few gigs at the Capitol and the Top Rank – Procol Harum, Kevin Ayers, the Boomtown Rats, the Clash and Patti Smith.

But the second I left school I knew I was off. Off to London where punk rock was happening, where the first British McDonalds had just opened, where life was.

A year in London, though, and I was frazzled, exhausted from sleeping on floors and living on beer and crisps. And so I was coming home for a rest, a recharge. And also to hook up with the Cardiff music scene.

Up in London I'd been writing a fanzine, a DIY magazine devoted to the only three bands that myself and my friend Charles thought worthy of our approval (Scritti Politti, The Fall and The Raincoats, in case you were wondering).

I had ideals coming out my ears. I thought big record companies were the Great Satan. I thought decentralisation and the democratisation of the means of production were essential. I thought everyone should form a band and sing songs about destroying the record business and put them out as singles pressed up on homemade pressing plants in our front rooms, using recycled shoes to make the vinyl.

And, actually, thinking about it now I'm not even sure I was wrong. All I know is I don't have the energy for that kind of commitment any more.

Anyway, I was writing this fanzine and had these quaint and angry beliefs, and as it happened I was not alone. There were people up and down the country espousing these same notions, people from all manner of nowhere towns who were inspired by punk rock to think they could actually do something for themselves. Which, in Britain, generally meant forming a band and sending your single to John Peel. And one of these bands was called Reptile Ranch, and they were from Risca in the Valleys and had just moved to Cardiff. They had seen my fanzine *After Hours* because I had left some copies of it in Spillers Records when I was down visiting my parents, and they wrote to the address, which was my ex flatmate's ex-girlfriend's sister's house in Holloway, and eventually the letter got to me. Now, fresh from the Magic Bus, I was going to visit them at their address in Splott.

Splott was somewhere I knew of, but had never consciously been in my life, part of the across-the-tracks Cardiff. The flat was in the upper half of a building that's no longer there, opposite a dismal pub called the Ruperra that's no longer there either, and a social club, the New Fleurs, which is still there, and back then was mostly patronised by steelworkers spending their redundancy money from East Moors, the steel mill that had up till lately been round the corner.

I rang the doorbell and a feller called Simon answered the door, looked terrified to see me and led me into an upstairs living room full of music equipment and a partially dismantled motorbike.

Turned out Simon was the keyboard player in Reptile Ranch, and he was about the shyest person I'd ever met. After a while I suggested going to the pub and he looked alarmed but grateful at the notion of movement, so we went to the Roath Cottage on Sanquhar Street, just by the house where Trezza Azzopardi's *The Hiding Place* is set, and I drank beer in the afternoon, because back then I drank beer any time I could, and Simon most likely had a half of cider and black, and the time passed slowly, and then we went back to the flat and met the other members of Reptile Ranch, Phil the bass player and Spike the guitarist, and Spike the guitarist's new girlfriend Lisa, and their landlord, Hywel the undertaker, who was a little older and a little more comfortable with the ways of the world. He had a small proto-synthesiser on which he made space invaders noises and intoned bleak poetry under the *nom de guerre* of Test To Destruction.

Anyway, for all their initial shyness, Reptile Ranch turned out to be industrious folk. Not only had they just put their own single out, they were busy organising a compilation album of like-minded Cardiff bands which they were planning to release on their own Z Block records. And that very evening there was going to be a meeting of all the bands concerned, if I fancied coming along.

Which I did, and soon we headed off in a mini crocodile over the metal footbridge off Sanquhar Street, past the prison and into town, where we made for Grassroots coffee bar, a centre for unemployed teenagers on the ground floor of a Charles Street townhouse.

This was the Factory, the Hacienda, the Roxy Club, the CBGBs, the veritable Cavern of Cardiff's DIY music scene. And that evening they were all there – Addiction from Aberdare, solvent-eyed punkers from a dying valley; Mad Dog from Merthyr (at first I actually thought their name was Mad Dog From Merthyr which would have been even better), who were a heavy metal band the way the MC5 and Motorhead were heavy metal bands. There was

Beaver – older blokes who'd taken a beat-up old bus from Aberystwyth to Warsaw and back playing cranked-up r&b; the New Form, squeaky-voiced students whose drummer was the first of my contemporaries to die; and there were the Riotous Brothers from Cardiff whose singer was a huge bloke called Dave, who's into civil war re-enactment these days.

And then there were the Young Marble Giants. Just by looking at them you could see they were the stars of the bunch. There were two brothers who were enormously tall – one wore a sailor's cap and the other had a crop with one single lock of hair stuck up like an antenna at the front – and the third member was a girl in a fifties dress. After the meeting Stuart, the one in the sailor's cap, gave me a tape. Later on I went back to my parents' house and listened to the Young Marble Giants tape in the dark and heard music that, to this day, doesn't sound like anything else – Kraftwerk fronted by a girl singing to herself at a bus stop might give you a vague idea.

That was it. I was sold on coming back to Cardiff. That summer I camped on Reptile Ranch's floor next to the motorbike, helped get the LP pressed up and taken to the distributors in London. I gave a copy to Geoff Travis of Rough Trade records, who decided to sign the Young Marble Giants more or less on the spot, which was lucky as they were on the point of splitting up.

I decided to form a band with a feller called Andr who was Reptile Ranch's manager, more or less. Andr played bass, I played guitar and sang, even though I was entirely unqualified to do either. I knew three chords on the guitar but I couldn't play them cleanly and had no idea how to combine them, so mostly I just played single notes in extremely ponderous sequences.

We went to Grassroots to hang out, dine on Twixes and cups of tea, listen to the baby punks play Sex Pistols records on the jukebox, gawp at the teenage Italian sisters from Rumney with the pictures of Siouxsie Sioux on the backs of their jackets, and to see the bands play.

Reptile Ranch played an improvised gig there to an audience of half a dozen bemused bystanders. Test To Destruction made a tape loop of *Anarchy in the UK* and let it play for an hour before he came on stage and intoned Nico songs in German over the synthesiser blip. Mad Dog from Merthyr brought their full stage act down from the valleys and blew dry ice out onto Charles Street. Inside you could barely see that there were only ten people there.

We went to Spillers Records, we went to the Sarsaparilla Bar in the Morgan Arcade, we went to Kelly's in the Market to sell our old LPs and supplement the dole – none of us were working except Phil the bass player, who had a job in a printer's.

In the evenings we went to Chapter to watch *Taxi Driver* or *Performance* or late-night horror movies. At night we didn't do much except go the Fleurs and play bingo, because back then there was hardly anything to do at night in Cardiff. We went once or twice to the Great Western or the New Moon to listen to the r&b bands, but we didn't really appreciate them. The house band at the New Moon was called Tiger Bay. They were the ugliest bunch of reprobates you ever saw on a stage and yet – and this may well be something I've dreamed – I'm sure that in a previous incarnation they had been called April and were momentarily hyped as Wales' answer to the Bay City Rollers. Probably the NSPCC stepped in to save our pop kids from falling into the hands of these fellers.

Anyway, what I'm saying is that Cardiff in the punk rock years was not a jumping town. It had good pubs, real pubs, Brains pubs, the Salutation, the Vulcan, the Oak, the Cottage, the Arcade, the Greyhound – all of them gone or changed utterly except the Vulcan. But that was about it. Clubbing, in the sense we know it now, didn't exist. There was a disco called Bumpers in the Castle Arcade, Baker's Row down by the side of Howells, Monty's on Charles Street where the nurses went, and the Top Rank on Queen Street, but these were alien territory to us, the preserve of straight people.

This new Cardiff I'd landed in seemed to be a likeable but grey city. Then the Young Marble Giants got a gig at somewhere called the Casablanca Club – 'down the Docks' apparently. We would go, of course we would go. Just one question – where were the Docks?

It's hard to recall now just how much of an absence the Docks were to Cardiffians (especially, but not exclusively, middle-class Cardiffians like me). Somehow we managed to understand that Cardiff had docks, that its existence as a city was predicated on those docks, while never for a moment contemplating visiting them. I think the way we sold it to ourselves was by saying that Cardiff used to have docks, used to be a port city, used to have a colourful dockland community. But now we didn't. As if the Docks had been physically erased from the map and its people transported (which is, of course, pretty much what has happened since).

So, to take the apparently simple step of staying on the Number 9 bus past the Central Station and on to its ultimate destination – Docks – was in no way the straightforward mission it seemed. It was like getting on a Streetcar Named Desire or the Merry Pranksters' bus marked Furtha. Or, rather, it was like getting on a bus and asking for a ticket to the imaginary past.

Which had to be twenty-five pence well spent, so we tried it anyway.

The bus took us through the sixties housing estate we now refer to as Butetown, and dropped us off by a big Victorian dockside boozer called the Big Windsor – which had once housed a French restaurant where my grandparents used to go. We didn't know where the Casablanca Club was in these fabled Docks, so we asked the driver, who said he didn't know either, but a black girl our age said she'd show us and walked us round to the Casablanca which turned out to be a converted chapel on the edge of this grand Victorian square, but it wasn't open yet so she took us round to a pub called The Ship & Pilot, which was full of Docks people, and we were the subject of some brief interest on the part of these locals, who were the characteristic Docks mix of black and white but mostly in between. Which was a surprise too. It's hard to believe now that back then Docks people were still rarely seen above the bridge.

In the Casablanca there was reggae on the sound system and the smell of dope in the air. I felt like I'd come through the green door and found the forbidden Cardiff. Then the reggae stopped and the band started and this was the first time I'd seen the Young Marble Giants play live and they were magnificent. A drum machine, an organ, a bass and a voice, each of them more skeletal than the next, only the bass even hinting at anything you might associate with rock and roll. It was music that suggested there was a world of possibilities out there, that what we defined as pop music or punk or whatever was only a tiny fragment of what was possible, and that to achieve something new what was needed was not extraordinary technical skill but just some new ideas.

This was the great message of punk of course – not that everyone should have spiky hair and play short fast rock songs for the next thirty years but rather that you could take your future into your own hands. If you wanted to be in a band – fine, you started one up, pressed your own records. If you wanted to be a writer – fine too, you started your own fanzine, all you needed was access to a photocopier.

Anyway, after the gig, inspired by the music and by the venue, I decided this would be the perfect place to put on the post-punk bands I liked, so I went backstage and found the manager, a black guy called Karl who sat me down, passed me the largest spliff I'd yet seen, and listened as I burbled on about my plans for worldwide revolution via punk rock. And I felt for a moment as if I'd found my place.

I hadn't of course, not really. Nothing much came of my plans to turn the Casablanca into a punky reggae Mecca. In the end it was easier and cheaper to put bands on in Grassroots, or upstairs in the old Transport Workers' club in Millicent Street than in the Docks, and gradually my Cardiff settled into a deliberately grey quotidian existence.

Me and Andr formed a group called the Puritan Guitars with a couple of students called Jeff and Blair. We were studiously drab boys in army surplus shoes and Marks & Spencers sweaters. Our name was barely ironic: we didn't take drugs, hardly drank, just the odd pint in the Mitre, round the back of our flat in Riverside, or the Roath Cottage, over past Jeff's room in Cathays.

I haunted Frankie Johnson's second-hand store on the corner of Neville Street, bought samosas from Madhav's over the road, took back lemonade bottles for the change. Lived on chips and curry sauce and Findus frozen pancakes, signed on in Westgate Street, went to the job centre in Greyfriars Street which used to have no jobs at all, except for stints on the night shift at petrol stations miles from anywhere for seventy-five pence an hour.

It was, to be honest, the most miserable year of my life.

Then the Puritan Guitars went up to London and played a gig to an audience of the post-punk great and good. I watched them shake their heads and file out and was blessed with the disconcerting sensation of watching myself on stage as we played and thinking, This is truly terrible music, this is an idea that has run out of steam.

Afterwards I was depressed for a while, then relieved. The Puritan Guitars never played again (however, our single, should you ever encounter a copy, is bewilderingly collectible). I moved out of Riverside into a room in Jeff's student house in Cathays and I got a job in an anarchist printer's – the people who'd printed up the Puritan Guitars sleeves, as it happened. And I found myself edging into another subterranean Cardiff – the anarcho-lefty lands.

This was a world of big shared houses on Connaught and Claude, the 108 Bookshop in Salisbury Road, where shoplifters were threatened with bad karma, the Halfway pub on Cathedral Road, where Welsh speaking was still seen as a radical statement, not a passport to a job with S4C. I did my best to like it, this world, to appreciate its raft of good intentions, but in truth it was an awful, utterly unglamorous world of veggie stews, Peruvian knitwear and benefit bops which always ended up with everyone getting down to the Rolling Stones.

Glamour: that was what post-punks lacked, that's what anarcho-hippies lacked, that's what Cardiff lacked.

I wasn't the only person thinking this, of course. We all did. Suddenly we were tired of listening to the DIY racket. We wanted tunes and beats and nice clothes to wear. We went back to the Oxfam shops, this time looking for finery not camouflage. We bought records from Woolworths, cheap compilations of Motown and Atlantic and Stax. Jeff dug out the northern soul singles he'd kept hidden while he was a punk rock misery guts and taught us how to do back-flips. All we needed now was a place to go.

We went back to the Docks. We danced to reggae at the Casablanca and the Community Centre. Most of all we danced at the Casino Club on Bute Street. Or was it called Mel's? Or was 'Mel's' just what they called the upstairs room, where the new thing was happening?

The new thing was New Romantics – hairdressers and shop

boys and girls dancing to David Bowie. They'd found themselves this club in the Docks where they could come out to play. They didn't let us in at first till we learned to dress up properly – I was outraged then, can't blame them now – so we'd dance downstairs with the pissed-up hookers and the old fellers. We danced to the Jacksons and Kool And The Gang, back-flipping through the winter of '80 to '81, then walking back to Splott and Cathays through the ruins of East Tindall Street, climbing the skeletons of abandoned warehouses, the remnants of the old Docks that even we could see was on its last legs, its ramshackle charms an inspiration but not a possible home for the likes of us.

New Romanticism conquered the city, conquered the nation. We took the train to Newport on Thursday nights, Roxy/Bowie night at the Stowaway, where the Sex Pistols once played. We went to the Xanadu on Wood Street, Nero's by the New Theatre, anywhere Mark Taylor was playing the records. We drank in the Lexington and Toni's bar. We were after sophistication, but all we could find in Cardiff was a glimmer, an inkling of a world that seemed to be passing us by.

I wanted out. Cardiff was, in retrospect, just showing the first signs of coming out of its shell, but they weren't nearly enough for a twenty-year-old who felt like he'd spent the last couple of years in an open prison.

I bought a van. We rehearsed a busking act, and nine of us went to Paris to play music and live on croissants and wine. We said farewell to Cardiff with a gig supporting The Fall at the Students' Union, and I pointed the blue Sherpa van towards the M4 and thought I'd never come back.

A STAIN ON THE MAP

Lloyd Robson

for tôpher mills, amongst others

so this is my home. this morose dump this castle ground this
moggy swamp this swab of land this marsh growth this tamponing
town of urban blood & brown this festering hole this rising damp i
keep running from & sloping back & insist on calling my home
whether it wants me or not so this is what it's all about.

i could so easily claim elsewhere. so easily claim cwmbran,
monmouth, plymouth, herefordshire – each accepts me as one of
their own. i could so easily go elsewhere could so easily claim
british the empire state ich dien ich bin ein european i am of the
continent introduce myself as a citizen of the world community the
globe the planet could so easily be permanently mentally abroad &
out of here cut loose from static.

sometimes i do, i describe myself as such. sometimes as welsh,
more often just cardiff. kahdiff. more often than that: roath or
splott or adamsdown – a delicate answer depending upon the city-
grasp held by the listener the questioner the other side how precise
do you want me to be exactly ay? come on now gimme a chance.
place of birth: st david's hospital. on my birth certificate cardiff
gets mentioned eight times; wales not once.

roath splott adamsdown. not a triangle renowned for its miracles
not a triangle at all; a linear grasp a rasp of frictional existence &
tender hammered attitude. i am from none of them, yet all. my
family from adamsdown & tremorfa; adamsdown when it was part
of roath. splott what i get accused of like it's something to be
ashamed of by those from the city's west or north. this side of the

95

bridge so not splott at all, but within the call of the splotlands' last orders a pint of dark don't mind if i thanks very much ta iechyd da 'ware teg down the hatch & up yours butty bach you-arr en shovel it down ya neck then pal.

so i am not from, but of. or rather: essentially, not entirely, from. i am a cardiff boy but this does not encapsulate does not define completely myself nor my experience we are both more. signed myself up for a lifetime of explanatory notes. the place i was born but did not school. the place i called home but had no permanent roof. the place of my family, but the ground too sodden to hold deep roots – beyond the past of grandparents heritage ceases to exist, of my migration there is no proof.

my accent is a shambles – i admit it readily; a just reflection of my loose view. it is the only map to my existence but there are too many contours leaving listeners confused. i will not deny my range my diversions; one minute cardiff st german's, the next plymouth st jude's. i've confessed to both in my own voice so they deserve to be heard.

i have reversed my father's attitude. as with so many of my parents' age, they fought to lose their cardiff accents to become acceptable in vocal range angle & rasp. we are regaining it on their behalf. i doubt they will appreciate this so i will explain to those dead & alive: cardiff today does not need to be ashamed of how it speaks of its many accents. the city will begin to accept itself for what it is before it can expect others to value it. we have a magnificent range of voices & accents. the beauty of how we think & speak. communication, after all, should be about what is said & not how. to judge a speaker on their accent, to base their value their class on how they sound, to balance whether we listen or not, to create abstract hierarchies based on vocal intonations & musical patterns, is to create inefficient ineffective irrelevant communication & true dysfluency – but on the listener's part. is to insult. my parents did not realise this, nor did those so many of their age who did & continue to do the same. they simply wished to play on a level playing field. so do i, but home not away. there is no need to unnecessarily limit the kahdiff experience; do not deny us our claims to diversity, we got range – it's the modus operandi the success the style the soul the truth, ruth, the kahdiff accent a myth perpetuated by those who would distance us from the couth – if you reckon they talks the same in ely as they duzz in tremorfa you're revealing your ignorance your ear ain't in tune. we got it & we got every right to keep it. it ain't english, it ain't cymraeg, but iss kahdiff welsh, true.

any road, wad da fuck do i know? i could be from anywhere. have: no stock, no tradition, no bloodline, no history. industrial migration my seven seas, my winds of change, my home nation. i have no idea of where the world considers me from; have no history no map of birth & death of pregnancy in-, or multi-racial, breeding tribal leaving marital political association power brokering escape from civil war social rebellion exodus from famine no tall tales handed down through generations old enough to leave them buried no telltale throwback idiosyncrasies no limp no hump no shock flash of colouring nothing nothing to give me signs to tell me from where the world considers me, my only compass broke & stumped & set to the east of queen street cobbing the hot dog of newport road.

such freedom. such liberty. but still, a magnet with the strength to suck me from pleasurable existence elsewhere in the universe the drag of my supposed home. i've left claw marks in the stone the rock the sand the snow each of them directed to my front door to the front doors of cardiff to the front doors of tremorfa splott cathays adamsdown roath to the front doors of tweedsmuir & canada roads the front doors of fairoak the front doors of emerald street sapphire street ruby & pearl to the front doors of properties bulldozed to the doors of nora to the maternity wards of st david's hospital & the corner of glossop road i've battered down them all they have all been home sometimes i was dragged by my own force & control kicking & screaming gnashing on yale keys & mortise locks but once inside i was of them; loved & in their hold. family. home.

perhaps we had it once: our family history. perhaps we couldn't afford its upkeep, pawned it, swapped it, drowned it down the toilet like me uncle john's parrot before he went back to practising the trumpet, dropped it getting off the bus like a baby's spouted cup full of warm tea, got drunk & left it in the pub, stashed it up the chimney in the newly weds' flat, perhaps it was sawn into strips & lengths & planks at a sanquahar street timber yard or buried under the parky's house in a llanrumney public park, perhaps it's been warped played down exposed mutated mutilated exaggerated to such an extent that we have forgotten what it was we were talking about, perhaps we ate it in a fit of munchies, perhaps my invisible friend took it with him, perhaps the old pissed on it cried on it died on it rested upon it *'just half a cup lil'* spilt it chucked it over the side on a £10 one-way ticket to australia commissioned it enlisted it signed it up got it under contract press-ganged it into service launched it floated it sunk it depth-charged bombed torpedoed it perhaps we tugged it out of the dock perhaps it is swimming somewhere or lies at the bottom of the severn chained to a rock perhaps we drowned it at birth tied it up in a sack aborted it before it had chance perhaps it is still to be fertilised still ovary & sperm an excuse to get down sweaty & turned on spent & done, perhaps clone or test-tube borne, perhaps it lies in the tip of a condom floating upon roath park lake waiting to choke a pintail a pochard a shoveler a wigeon a tufted an escaped ruddy shelduck or down the canal with the bridge-livers the taff with the jumpers the waders the face down drunk perhaps we couldn't bear it at all perhaps the weight of it broke our back perhaps it is left in a doorway somewheres to be brought up by fosterers front page of the echo & renamed by staff perhaps it puffs at a mouth organ & sits by a hat perhaps it is shafted on scrumpy jack perhaps we are running running running from it fast as we can perhaps it is hiding waiting to jump us when we're fool enough to relax & consider the future ours, clean pure of its influence in blue skies calm seas & sunrise yes, perhaps it is that.

me: i hunt the city for it. with the worst result. to redefine an allegory to redirect an analogy from robert bolt's 'man for all seasons' to fuck about & feed off a conversation between william roper & sir thomas more: i chopped down every tree i saw in search for it, kicked over wheely bins, swore down alleys, promised i'd get it, uprooted floorboards, spat down cellars, hid in attics, broke windowpanes & scattered the shards & fragments poked my nose into graffiti'd lockups sprayed my stench along the crumbling plaster walls so it could follow my scent know i was on its tail its case on the look-out so it could catch me up & hunt me down, i bothered the boys & annoyed the old locals i peered through lace curtains i opened top drawers & boxes on wardrobes i prodded & probed i misconstrued & got it all wrong i forced them to give it to me straight just as it happened i told them my side to get to theirs i embarrassed myself with the tales they remembered of me as a child i led them down alleys so long since they visited so long so old i took a boat out to sea i went egging in marsh nests & disturbed the birds in their webbing the mud in its bedding i woke up the coast & the city i telexed telephoned telegrammed emailed wrote letters postcards took photographs collected party snaps & weddings framed by confetti & the steps of a church i faxed fucked & became well fed always staying for tea well while i'm here i may as well i built up the evidence my case file was bulging i was cutting the forest pressing the paper & creating the backlog & eventually, when the city was bare & all was there for me to see & feel & grasp between my sweaty grabbing mitts, the very worst happened: i found it. or it found me. i grinned at it hid from it towered overshadowed me & now it's hounding me chasing me & i have nowhere left to hide for i chopped down everything in search of it & now on the concrete the tarmac it has clamped me & i am immobile i am whip-tied lashed lasso & lariat & it drags me back in its roy rogers t-shirt it drags me down down o clever me, o driven me, o me in search of myself & my city, now it has found me what do i do with it what does it do with me? for my debt for the debt of my family i repay with interest upon interest compounded in bankruptcy for the rest of my lifetime. my search, my family, my history, my city. i had to go find it didn't i; wouldn't leave it be. dozy fuckin idiot. me me me.

& frankly now i'm furious with my meddling, with my insistence my arrogance my stubborn determination to define it for myself i just had to do it & you know what you know what i am now faced with? i'm faced with the fact i fucking hate it. i hate it with all my heart. i hate it with the draw of history the backward arc the denial of the future my future any future apart from the one which emerges here right now in street light & bus lane, brass fire sets & green tile porches, in all day opening sunday shops, in petrol stat & pub, brains house & labour club, worker's terrace & dole flat, in children unrolling fag butts outside the shops on harris avenue, in the mustard on the tongue for swearing too young, in fingering the railings, in fish on fridays, in a pack of fresh cockles, pepper & vinegar, whelks, chitterling, bread pudding, welsh cakes, irish cakes, clarpie, bacon sarnies from roches in the market. in the grumpy old fucker who ran the hayes island tea bar, in the hayes without st david's, the open air market, tattoo at the castle, traffic on queen street, day trips to merthyr mawr & barry, in the IRA slogan painted on the wall of the old library opposite howell's – years it stayed, in the latent religious bigotry still simmering under the cardiff irish surface, in dirty priests, ex-footballers running pubs & rugby club politicians, in the self-made men, in the housewives, the welsh & asian & african mams, in the rule books, the grand plans, the us & them, the eucharist of christ & in the multitudinous eyes of god systematically poked out one by one, in walking down st mary's street me little hand in me dad's.

but i cannot do anything about this, for to hate this city is to hate myself so i will just have to shoulder it like the grown man i failed to notice i have finally become; the grown man i claim i am, & clam up. cos most of all i hate it because i love it! love it! love it so! but why should anywhere be so important to me why should i deny myself the freedom of movement of an open mind of a right to claim citizenship of the whole world why do i limit myself with an environment which has drugged me up & dragged me down on which i've been puffing & choking since 1969 why should i take on the attitudes of this miniscule part of the universe why did i develop so?

the answer is nothing. nothing makes me put up with any of this, but neither do i have a choice. as much as i love it i despise it or rather i despise how i have come to perceive it what i have made it become. i despise the fact i've walked into the trap enrapt myself within my own history memory & need for reassuring security. i despise the fact it matters to me; despise the fact i need it so much it is my weakness my fetish my achilles.

but c'est la vie & all that. what little i think i know for certain was discovered at odd moments in me life: me nan is not really me nan; my parents' parents all remarried; my parents don't share the same parents as me uncles & anties; me father found himself the only proddy in a suddenly catholic family; me paternal grampy liked a drop of course; of me mam's parents all i remember is alleyways between the houses, blackberry picking at the back of their tremorfa garden legs cut to shreds; somewhere there's an uncle never raised never questioned nor discussed at length; occasionally i attend a funeral get introduced to plenty of people who remember me as a little dink, think i'm me brother, remember me parents or have no idea who i am; sometimes they comment i have the look of my father, i watch them drift to some distant past; my father couldn't leave this city fast enough, & that he kept coming back.

this city breaks my heart & holds my hand. rubs my nose in my own filth my own past my own extremes & limitations my own limp dysfluency my inability to speak to articulate communicate my own bad sound. it haunts me bullies me slaps me about. it pulls me around gives me chinese burns when i ain't playing no more & wanna go & sulk. it puts me down humiliates me in public but then, when no one's looking, drags me back up, strokes my hair, gives me a clip round the ear, tells me i deserved that now stop being such a little tit & get on with life, be a man.

so what of this city? what the fuck's it gota do wi me? it's a simple reply: kahdiff's presence the only geographical historical cultural & personal constant in my life; wherever we lived i was always i was always from cardiff, i was not allowed to nor did i want to forget this fact.

this city a minefield, i risk explosions from my younger life when all i'm trying is to get from A to B or buy an echo, a loaf, a pint. but ultimately inevitably obviously i love desire am addicted to these little bombs they engage me with my past a past so often so easily so previously lost or forgotten about.

kahdiff flash past: the bus depot on newport road opposite the rover bridge; tremorfa front room covered in newspaper & pots of airfix; walking down clifton & pearl from st german's after a choirboy porthcawl coney beach camp trip; houses full of kids; waiting outside the ninian park changing rooms – autographs from dwyer, ronson, grapes; the satdees when me uncle would take me to a match, breaking down on the eastern bypass in his rover one hundred, still making the game by going with his father, standing in the grange end, glorying in a buchanan hat trick & the 4-0 drubbing of sheffield united on a birthday; losing to brooking's west ham on another; wales beating the czechs 1-0 on ratcliffe's first cap; ronnie moore scoring & me uncle geoff saying that's twice in my presence, now i'd have to attend every match.

a reality of touchstones, won't leave me alone, haunting us dragging us forth & back. i have lost so many memories of this city, find myself blasted to the past walking down streets turning corners looking up or down, kneeling to tie a shoelace being faced with a perspective not experienced since childhood getting it all come flooding back. mental & emotional explosions relived in the city, ourselves & our mutual pasts incessantly & irresistibly layering us folding us under a blubbering belly of insight & experience as we stomp around headphones on or plastered drunk or sober & in a rush suffocating & breathing life reminding us of fights & piss ups & snogs & lust, humilities & hangovers, dancing swinging swearing reading writing on lamp-posts swearing & loving & sulking & kicking off *what the fuck did you mean by that?!* crying in the streets on the way back to someone's house if not my own trying to apologise trying to make up. child & adult. not much different after all this time. knowing everything, reading the footprints, the smells in the wind, the hang of the stars, finding myself & getting lost.

& still the city reveals itself. elephants on queen street, the market's neon clock, twisted chimney pots, the half white brick wall above sam's bar with its ghosts of outline from previous neighbours & architectural pasts, purpose, life, the stained glass, the worlds on offer over upstairs sills & old warped panes *LOOK OUT! UP!* – as teenagers, pushing a girlfriend into the door of floyd's clothing she thinking i'd gone mad or dangerous vicious malicious, seconds later the pavement cracks a falling pane of glass. *how did you know that would happen?* she asked. you tune in & pick it up. it pumps the blood. cuts you open & fucks you up. keeps you bubbling, bouncing, tripping the gaps in the slabs. tune it in or get it smashed.

newport road. i remembers arguing with friends falling out with a girlfriend who when i lived in monmouth insisted on approaching the city on taking a route via north rather than the easterly newport road. did my fucking head in. furious rows in the car to the city. robbing me of my territory robbing me of that feeling of recharging refuelling once again becoming assimilated & knowing where i am, of what, of being at one with my city, robbed me blind & set me off on a bad storm cloud mood building the continuation of association between cardiff & me as a stroppy bastard. denying me a trip through my homeland. worse: her saying it didn't matter; claiming north road was a nicer route. cheeky bleedin cow. the royal oak. the turn to leo's. from then on i demanded i always do the drive to cardiff. she would fume, sensing a loss of class & control. doesn't seem so long ago. i like to think i'm calmer now. but then, these days, i get my fix daily.

clifton street. cobblers, butchers, clark's chippy, tony's la gondola caff. more bacon than a pig ranch. roath cop shop: you don't see the police but you see their cars; once got bombed, made it onto ceefax. the now gone offy on the corner with copper street: old brains sign painted out; little counter, back room, floor stacked with crates of flagons, old woman surrounded by beer; empties & money back. the clifton pub: my old local, jim reeves & elvis, i came here when me father past had a pint of dark to mark his time to mark his gas-filled last gasp. his old man used to drink in the bertram, he would have to go fetch him; bring him back. i'd drink the old arcade with mine. phoned me uncle to tell em the news, went round theirs to see hear me anty cry.

cardiff was is a surrogate dad. father & son aren't meant to always stand shoulder to shoulder see eye to eye without some kind of poker stare friction some kinda punchy rub some kind of man to man don't push your luck what you staring at a desire to prove something to each other the worm that turned you might have your wind up but i'm still your old man don't you go forgetting that lad.

cardiff a city of characters, saints, family, cunts & thugs. a conglomerate of dealers movers & small-time crime. masons, councillors, committees, street gangs. this threatening to be something else aping the appearance of a big city plan this yokohama of the north this post-industrial urbanity this reclaimed land this ten year redevelopment this multi-racial dog end this dock of ash this phlegm & accent stuck dug in the throat gobbing off & gagging on. give me the last drag on that then boy before i tells ya old man. what you should've but didn't or shouldn't have done. everything you make of it & less & more. move it in & ship it out. this home patch this scrag of life this capital this potential this delicate fanning of the flames gimme a match so watch out smart arse it's all coming back. raise the canopy build the woods the words let loose the undergrowth the camouflage give me something somewhere where i can once again get lost give me something to shout about face the wall count to one hundred gimme a chance to hide myself to lose myself to forget what i know to redefine to cut new tracks to get out there boy get planting digging to sharpen the city to hone the focus to reload the camera to lick my pencil to blunt the axe. cardiff as rumbling creative stove & store? too fuckin right. take me back.

Branch	Date
no	11/04